WHERE THE
STREAM RAN RED

For Muriel, as always,
and for our children and grandchildren with
the hope they will never lose a sense of where,
in part at least, they spring from

WHERE THE STREAM RAN RED

Memories and Histories of a Welsh Mining Valley

SAM ADAMS

The publishers wish to acknowledge the support of
Cyngor Llyfrau Cymru

Cover photograph: Wyndham Jones Collection
Cover design: Y Lolfa

ISBN: 978 1 78461 118 7

Published and printed in Wales
on paper from well-maintained forests by
Y Lolfa Cyf., Talybont, Ceredigion SY24 5HE
website www.ylolfa.com
e-mail ylolfa@ylolfa.com
tel 01970 832 304
fax 832 782

The Williams family from the Vale of Glamorgan

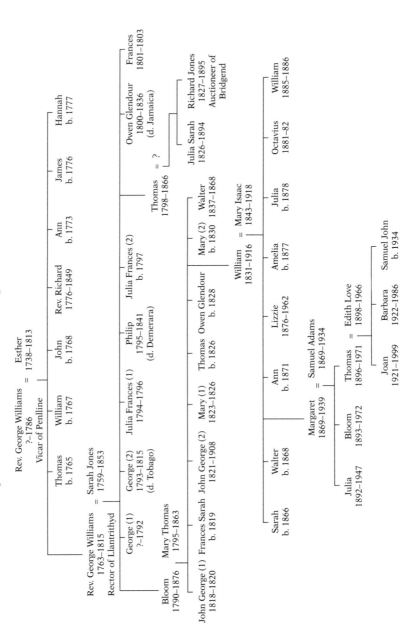

Descendants of William Adams of Newhall, Derbyshire

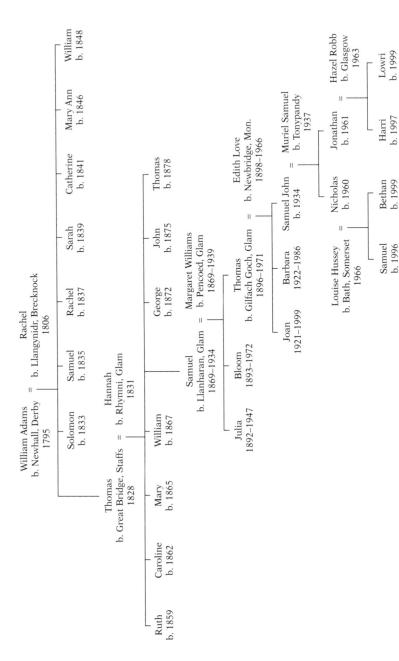

The Lewis connection and the Loves, my mother's family

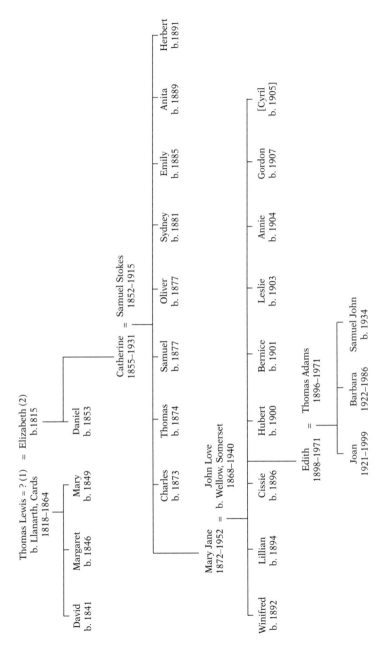

Thomas Lewis = ? (1)   =   Elizabeth (2)
b. Llanarth, Cards   b.1815
1818–1864

David   Margaret   Mary   Daniel
b. 1841   b. 1846   b. 1849   b. 1853

Catherine   =   Samuel Stokes
1855–1931   1852–1915

Charles   Thomas   Samuel   Oliver   Sydney   Emily   Anita   Herbert
b. 1873   b. 1874   b. 1877   b. 1877   b. 1881   b. 1885   b. 1889   b. 1891

John Love
b. Wellow, Somerset
1868–1940

Mary Jane
1872–1952

Winifred   Lillian   Cissie   Hubert   Bernice   Leslie   Annie   Gordon   [Cyril
b. 1892   b. 1894   b. 1896   b. 1900   b. 1901   b. 1903   b. 1904   b. 1907   b. 1905]

Edith   =   Thomas Adams
1898–1971   1896–1971

Joan   Barbara   Samuel John
1921–1999   1922–1986   b. 1934

7

Preface

ON THE OS map Gilfach resembles nothing so much as a lasso and, no matter how distant from it I may be in time and place, I am caught in the noose. It tugs me back to my beginnings and I am gently held.

Gilfach Goch is the name of a valley and the village that occupies it. It differs from many other coalfield settlements in this respect. Visitors entering the valley for the first time, if the weather is fair, will find it pleasant to look upon. They will take the only road, along the eastern flank – and where, quite soon, the housing thins out and there is an open prospect to the left, they will see ragged hedges marking the boundaries of fields on the opposite low green hill and a long diagonal of trees climbing towards the south. These provide shade to a path, the Rhiw, leading to farms just over the brow. And below, at the bottom of the valley, if they are travelling slowly or, better still, on foot, they should catch a glimpse of the river, which is clear on a stony bed. Almost in the middle of the valley, alongside the river, is a small grassed area that is freakishly more or less flat. We used to call it 'the *cwm*' and we played football there. Overlooking the *cwm* from the west is a barn-like building of pink brick with a corrugated roof. It is the very last structure belonging to the time when Gilfach was a mining valley, the stables of 'the Squint', the drift mine where my father was an electrician. The stables once housed the horses that hauled the drams underground and must still have some use, if not as a stable, to have survived.

Soon, around a bend in the road, near the beginning of a long High Street, the top of the valley is revealed, where the mountains crowd around steeply above the remaining terraces both sides of the river. Straight ahead to the north an almost symmetrical low hill, like a squashed bell curve, rises above the general level of the mountain. From below it appears an easy climb, but it is not. At the top is a concrete plinth, a trig point, showing the height is 416 metres, some 1,360 feet. All about you is the moor, stretching on and on to the north and west, where the infant trickle that will become the Ogwr Fach, Gilfach's river, rises amid boggy pools and cotton grass. But to the east, within a few hundred yards, is the edge of a steep descent into the neighbouring valley, Clydach Vale, an offshoot of the Rhondda. You can sidle carefully down from the highest point, as perforce you clambered up, or simply step onto a grassy slope so abrupt that within two paces you find yourself running to keep your balance and unable to stop until the mountain relents. Narrow sheep tracks skirting the quarries will bring you down again to road.

The valley bottom is 600 feet above sea level. This is a rainy place. The rains come usually from the west and, at home from a front window, I often saw them on the other side of the valley approaching down the narrow cleft that marks the course of a brook, the Abercerdin, which used to be dammed in the summer for bathing on sunny days. Near the mountain wall at the top of the valley the riverside area is now green and slopes smoothly to the stream, which runs without a kink. It is curiously featureless, as though hollowed out. And that is what has happened. In this part of the valley, for almost a century, coal was mined intensively. In the 1970s what remained of collieries and slagheaps was swept away and the valley floor purged not only of all evidence of industry, but also, inevitably, of its original shape, before the pits were sunk. Then, it must have been beautiful indeed, with natural woodland filling much of the valley floor either side of the winding river, bracken-clad lower slopes and the rougher, variegated greens of enclosing mountains above to the level of the moor. Two decades of mining had already polluted the river and ripped apart the green fabric of the upper valley when, sometime between 1877 and 1881, my father's grandparents moved to

Gilfach Goch with all their children and chattels. By the time my mother's parents arrived, after 1911, driven perhaps by the violent unrest of that period, the industrialisation of the valley was complete.

The road, baulked by the mountain at the top of the valley, bends decisively, crosses the river and heads down the western side. There, beyond the pine ends of a ragged fringe of terraced houses was the elementary school, named Abercerdin after the brook close by. From the school, in my young days, the road ran straight across the valley to join with High Street the other side, very near the house where I was born, so closing the loop.

One

I FIRST MET Muriel, who three years later would become my wife, at The Library in Llwynypia. This Library was not the usual book-lined space frequented by students; it was a popular dancehall. More properly, it was the Miners' Institute, a large double-fronted building, set back from the road that ran from Tonypandy on up the Rhondda Fawr to Treorci. Built for and maintained by contributions from the hundreds of miners who worked a stone's throw away in the Llwynypia pits, it housed amenities for the leisure and self-improvement of the men and their families. In the sloping garden at the front of the institute was a larger than life-size bronze statue of Archibald Hood, a Scottish mining engineer, who, despite geological problems, persisted in sinking shafts in what had been until then, in the early 1860s, meagre farmland. Climbing the steps on our way to the dance we passed by Hood, heavily bearded and supported by a cane, pointing dramatically towards the Llwynypia Number One Pit, sunk in 1863 – not the first in the Rhondda valleys, but the inauguration of their industrial transformation.

When, at the end of the dance, I asked Muriel if I could walk her home, I did not think where that would lead, in the short term or the long. She said she had come to the dance and would go home with a friend who lived in the next street. But to my surprise she agreed to see a film with me the following week, though not in Tonypandy, as I expected. She would come to Gilfach Goch, my home village, a five-penny bus ride off and not part of the Rhondda at all. Will Samuel, her father, thought this a bad idea. 'You be careful, my girl,' he said, intending more than the usual cautionary advice of father to teenage daughter, 'they're a funny lot over there.'

It was true there had been two murders in Gilfach within a couple of months not long before. I was away in Aberystwyth when they occurred and learned about them later from my Roberts cousins who, as the local ambulance drivers, had been called to the dreadful scenes. One was the climax of years of domestic violence, when the cowed and beaten wife had at last turned against her brutish husband and blasted him with his own shotgun while he slept. The other I felt more keenly. Down from university, relaxing between sets of tennis in the shade of the pavilion veranda on warm summer days, from time to time my friends and I watched a young woman pushing a pram along the paths of the children's park over the fence. She had long fair hair and was sensuously proportioned, a blonde pin-up. If the park were quiet, as was usual on school days, she would leave the pram by a bench and sit on one of the swings and swing herself to and fro, not very high but high enough for the breeze of her motion to trail her long blond hair behind and lift her skirt to her thighs as she arced down. I think she was unaware of our presence, and in a little while would return to the pram and her solitary walk. Memory, I know, is elaborated on primary recollection and plays us false, but that image seems to me as clear now as when I first saw her, in some trance of recollection of her own perhaps, swinging on the children's swings in the Welfare Park. One night a boyfriend, maddened by who knows what, attacked her on the doorstep of the house where she lived with her mother, slashing at her with a knife until (my cousins said) her blood spurted up the wall of the painted and polished front porch.

The murders did not give Gilfach its bad reputation, or not them alone. To many outsiders, who had never been there, it was a rough place, a backward place. Rhondda friends would sometimes greet me with, 'How are the stagecoaches running these days?' As a mining village Gilfach was assumed to be a young upstart, far short of the advanced stage of civil society in the Rhondda. This was not wholly correct. George Yates's

1799 map of Glamorgan shows among the hills a tributary of the Ogwr Fawr, which it names Ogwr Fach, but it does not name the valley through which the young stream flows from its headwaters in the mountains beyond. It does, however, show coal pits. Half a century before any coal was mined in the Rhondda, some form of mining from drifts or shallow shafts was already taking place in the spot later maps name Gilfach Goch, 'Little Red Nook'. The origin of the name has been disputed. A romantic explanation has tribal Welshmen fighting Roman invaders on the mountains and winning a spectacular victory, so that the valley ran red with enemy blood. In my schooldays, the autumnal rusting of tall bracken that covered much of the hillside suggested another possibility. A third persuasively argues that the name, which on the earliest maps was attached to the mountain, indicated the narrowest part of the valley (*cil*), where the stream appeared red (*coch*) because it ran over iron ore-bearing rocks.

In the matter of the exploitation of coal measures contained in the great geological syncline stretching from west to east across south Wales, Gilfach then has historical precedence over the Rhondda. That, too, is interesting. Why, without thinking, do I make a comparison with the valleys of a different river system? The Ogwr Fach joins the larger Ogwr Fawr at Blackmill, about five miles south and west of Gilfach and from there the combined waters curve west again and flow through Bridgend, passing close by Pencoed, Coychurch and Merthyr Mawr (all three significant in the sliver of family history that has long fascinated me) before entering the waters of the Bristol Channel at Ogmore-by-Sea. Meanwhile, the Rhondda Fawr and Rhondda Fach, travelling in parallel, head south-east before meeting at Porth, whence the enlarged river continues in much the same direction until it meets the Taff at Pontypridd. From there it is another twelve miles to the coast at Cardiff, the width of the entire Vale of Glamorgan, almost twenty-five miles as the crow flies, from Ogmore. That is the truth of the map; but what really matters is the way the heads of the valleys lean together, so that the top of Gilfach is no more than a mile and a half from Tonypandy, if you walk over the mountain. It is a steep and rugged route, but one much frequented in the early days of mining. The same journey by bus or car, even now, is nine miles. Once in a while, as on those occasions when I missed the last bus, or memorably when Muriel trudged all the way through snow because there were no buses, we walked the road between our homes or, more rarely, trekked over the mountain. On light summer evenings, in fair weather, the latter was distinctly preferable.

When, in the 1860s, industrial development began in earnest, Gilfach was rapidly outstripped by the much larger Rhondda, where ribbons of settlement spooled out along the lower slopes of the hills above pits sunk in the valley floor, from Penrhiwfer to Williamstown to Penygraig to Tonypandy to Llwynypia and so on and on, one village merging imperceptibly with the next. The pace of industrial development in the Rhondda Fawr and Rhondda Fach was accompanied by rapid increase in population, from 951 in the entirely rural economy of 1851, to 16,914 at the 1871 census and 65,632 in 1881, bringing in its train the need for more and more houses, schools, chapels, churches, pubs, shops, sports clubs, civic institutions of all kinds, and roads and rail connections.

Compared to this sixteen-mile-long anthill with its seventy or more pits, the growth of Gilfach Goch, a minor cul-de-sac, was very modest. It is not a simple matter to calculate how many people lived in its scattered farms and dwellings in 1851, but they could be told in dozens rather than hundreds. In 1862, Evan Evans, a brewer and innkeeper from Merthyr, opened a mine on the western side of the Ogwr Fach, bringing an influx of Merthyr miners and their families with him, and in 1863 the sinking of a pit east of the river at the upper end of the valley by Archibald Hood's Glamorgan Coal Company accelerated change. By 1871, the mine owners had constructed 119 new houses for their workers, whose rents were deducted from earnings. They were mostly simple two-up, two-down dwellings built of local sandstone from quarries that scabbed the mountain. The quarries were a feature of the wonderful adult-free playground of our childhood. In one, I was struck by a flying stone in a friendly fire incident and had my bleeding scalp licked and tears stopped by Dash, George and Trevor's hairy black-and-white mongrel. That was the summer of 1943, and so efficacious were the dog's ministrations I am not sure my mother ever knew about it.

Hewn and dressed, the quarry stone quickly weathered dark grey-green in the coal-dust-laden rain, as I well remember, for those earliest terraces still stood almost a hundred years later. The houses were small and low with mean doors and windows, but there were solid roofs over the heads of miners and their families, with chimneys and fireplaces against the winter cold, better than the wooden huts they replaced. They had no other amenity. How could they – built in a wilderness, a rather beautiful wilderness perhaps, amid mountains and woods, and with a still clear stream nearby? All that soon changed, although a broad ribbon of natural woodland persisted down the western flank of the Ogwr Fach as late as 1900. Downstairs, the floors of the miners' cottages were of large stone slabs, sprinkled with sand for ease of cleaning. As a boy, I knew one of these dwellings, the home of Ray, a teenager who came and lived with us until he was eighteen and decided on national service in the army rather than a life in the pit. The slab floor in that house was not sanded. Moss and grass grew in the black earth between the stones, like green grouting, and chickens wandered in from the untended garden.

The population of Gilfach was 706 in 1871. The early census returns are difficult to interpret because enumeration was conducted on the basis of parishes, and Gilfach was not a parish. The pastoral care of the valley, in the state-sponsored Anglican tradition, was shared by three parishes – Llandyfodwg the western side, Ystradyfodwg the north-eastern corner, and Llantrisant the remainder of the eastern side. This ecclesiastical nonsense in turn influenced civil and administrative organisation. Even when Gilfach became a parish in its own right in 1924, the old tripartite parochial division continued to be reflected in local council and parliamentary constituency boundaries. When I was growing up there, the population of Gilfach was about 3,000. It is 2,500 now and was probably more when the coal industry was at its height and families were commonly larger than that at present. But whatever the official figure, the village was represented by three MPs and three local councils. One might think three of each should be more effective than one. Nothing could be further from the truth. Gilfach was always an afterthought to elected representatives whose major concerns lay elsewhere, and finding agreement between local councils about action to ameliorate conditions for those living in the valley was invariably protracted and difficult.

In 1871, a petition signed by twenty-four people of some standing in the emerging community, ministers of religion, colliery officials, shopkeepers, publicans, was addressed to 'the Magistrate of the County of Glamorgan':

> We the undersigned inhabitants of Gilfach Goch, in the several parishes of Ystradyfodwg, Llandyfodwg and Llantrisant, desire to petition you for the services of a resident policeman at Gilfach Goch. The place consists of about a hundred houses with a population amounting to about a 1,000. There are three places of worship, two schools, two collieries and five public houses.
>
> The place is three miles distant from Tonyrefail, where a policeman resides who now has Gilfach Goch within the limit of his beat. This distance is so great and the country between so irregular and dangerous for night travelling that the policeman can only be expected to come over occasionally and that during the day, a time when he is never required.
>
> The chief cause of this petition being made is the riotous and drunken conduct of those who seem to think that it is a place of refuge where they are free from all the restraints of Authority and Law.

In this depiction of what seems a remote outlaw territory we surely see a hint of the reputation that clung to Gilfach deep into the next century. How quickly the earnest request was granted I do not know. I recall clearly the local police of my boyhood, Sergeant Hobbs and Constable Jock Wilson, both impressively large. They patrolled the village day and night with a keen look and a nod for everyone. I was not aware of any rowdiness. It was widely known that inappropriate behaviour could be dealt with summarily, and in those days guilty parties took their punishment without complaint to higher authority. If a stranger appeared in the valley, within hours he would be approached and asked his name, address and business. Very little happened that Hobbs and Wilson did not know about.

Gilfach inhabitants in the nineteenth century faced more pressing concerns than rowdy drunkenness. The houses built by the coal companies did not have piped water, or even standpipes to serve a street. Water for daily use was taken from hillside springs. Much of it was of poor quality and the springs often dried up in summer. Sewerage was at best highly unsatisfactory. In 1881 there were no sewers in the valley and defective house drains voided their contents into the road. Many rural areas throughout the British Isles were as poorly served in these respects but did not share the same speed and density of population growth. It was not until 1896 that houses in the Llantrisant and Ystradyfodwg zones of the valley were connected to a main sewer, while Llandyfodwg waited still longer. That typhoid and cholera were not endemic is a miracle.

The first consideration of coal owners, once the viability of a mine had been established, was the construction of a railway line to carry the coal away, but they were not interested in roads. Having built houses near the pit so that the supply of labour was close at hand, roads were irrelevant. As the good people of the valley said in 1871, Gilfach Goch is about three miles from Tonyrefail – quite steeply uphill. I remember the gradient well. On 3 July in the same year the *Western Mail* reported a connecting road was to be built – not before time:

> Not very long ago, a horse and cart tumbled from the side of the mountain to the valley beneath. There are several hundreds of people living in the district, but, being mostly Welsh, they climb their old mountains without complaining, but when a horse fails to ape the goat, and misses his footing, they are reminded of the fact that a road would be better for the animal. It is true the railway reaches within a short distance of the village, but that is almost the only convenient way to the place; and to reach it from the Rhondda Valley, or Tonyrefail, the public must go by cart and compass, or follow the sheep tracks.

Conflict over the construction of the mile and a half of road completed by July 1872 involved landowners too. They had contributed to the costs, and to recoup their outlay erected tollgates where charges of between one shilling and half-a-crown were levied. This was only the beginning of troubles that rumbled on for decades.

An unwary traveller can easily pass along the road now labelled A4093, from Tonyrefail via Blackmill to Bridgend, without noticing the junction and the sign pointing north into the dead-end valley. The junction is marked in the 1900 Ordnance Survey (1:10,560) map, but the road north continues little more than a quarter of a mile before petering out in a track marked with a dotted line before disappearing altogether. Here and there higher up the valley, where the pits and most of the housing are located, short bits of road are more confidently indicated (along with the GWR rail line), but most of the valley is served by paths beaten by workers and their families on their essential journeys. An enlarged postcard photograph of a short stretch of what became known as High Street, Gilfach's main road – including the house where I grew up – shows this thoroughfare as broad as it is today, but still roughly surfaced with loose limestone compacted in parts by the passage of vehicles. That was about 1913. The 1921 OS map still shows no road around the top of the valley, although there are rows of houses, most of which had stood for half a century. And it remained impossible for a vehicle to travel by road to the western side of the valley, although by then what had become known as Evanstown, after Evan Evans, the mine owner, had sprouted close-packed terraces.

Evanstown terminated at Coronation Road, only two hundred yards from a link with High Street on the eastern side, but separating them as effectively as a high wall was a line on the map labelled 'Parly. Co. Div., Union & U.D. By.', which means Parliamentary Constituency Division, [Poor Law] Union and Urban District Boundary. The idea of building a road across this artificial division, and over the river and the railway, which also stood in the way, had been first mooted in 1890. In 1920 it was raised again and eventually the expense was shared between the councils concerned. The plan involved channelling the river through a culvert over which an embankment was built largely of colliery waste, slag and still-glowing clinker from the steam-driven colliery engine house. The macadamised road topped the embankment, at the blunt end of which a steel bridge crossed the railway line, to join a stubby offshoot of High Street the other side. Construction took almost five years and cost £18,000. Even after this exceedingly protracted development, the public service buses of the Rhondda Transport Co. needed a terminus near the end of High Street and another in Evanstown. It was only in the 1930s that the road around the top was completed and it became possible to make a circuit of the valley in a motor vehicle. No wonder the jibe about stagecoaches running to Gilfach was current in the 1950s. For all I know it may still be so.

The settlement of the valley was largely completed by Welsh Garden Cities Ltd, a company set up to bring this concept in modern urban development to Wales. In 1910, to the east of the Ogwr Fach, at the hitherto empty lower end of the valley, it built streets of semi-detached houses with bathrooms and fireplaces which had back boilers to heat the water, and gardens – small squares at the front behind railings, larger at the back for cultivation. They made a grand contrast with the older terraces at the top of the valley. On the 1921 OS map this new housing is labelled Gilfach Garden Village, but it is known locally as Garden City or, more usually, the City, and most of the people who moved in there were newcomers. A number of the streets run quite steeply down the valley side to the railway line, and several were given arboreal names, like Oak, Elm and Ash, although the last, only a hundred yards from the junction with the A4093, was Thomas Street, where Joan, my sister, lived in the early years of her marriage. A Red & White bus ventured into the valley as far as the top of Thomas Street and passengers for Bridgend or further west made sure they were there in good time to catch it, because the service was infrequent. That was where, as a student, I began my all-day journey to Aberystwyth.

Throughout my boyhood and beyond the Rhondda Transport Company's red buses carried the great majority of Gilfach's travelling public where they usually wanted to go – to Tonyrefail (where passengers were dropped a brisk walk away from the Cardiff bus stop), or to Penygraig and Tonypandy, which were busy shopping centres. It was a half-hourly service. In 1914, the year that saw the completion of the Garden City project, the first vehicles on this route (and this shakes me) were electrically operated. They were what we later termed 'trolleybuses', actually adaptations of the tramcars the company ran along tracks in the Rhondda, but drawing their power from wires suspended from posts at the side of the road. The apparent oddity of electricity being available when much else, by modern standards, seemed still primitive is easily explained: electricity had already been introduced into mining. Quickly perceiving the value of electrical lighting and power – not least for the pumps, hitherto steam driven, in mines prone to flooding – mine owners and companies invested in electricity generating plants. Spare capacity they sold to other users, such as the Rhondda Bus Company and business premises. The Powell Duffryn Coal Company was the largest producer of electricity in south Wales before the First World War, and with other colliery and private operators generated more than half the electrical power for general use into the 1930s. There was nothing altruistic about this; it was to increase profits. Although electrical machinery of increasing power and sophistication had been employed in the Cambrian Colliery in Clydach Vale for almost half a century, lighting in houses overlooking the pit still relied upon town gas, oil lamps and candles into the 1940s, as Muriel, whose home was in that valley, remembers. In Gilfach Goch, the Welsh Navigation Steam Coal Company supplied power for community lighting. There was no town gas and the wiring of houses to receive electric lighting was a great boon. In the 1920s, it kept my father, a colliery electrician, busy in his spare time, to the advantage of the small family business established by his father.

In the century 1850–1950, much of what was good and all that was bad about life in the south Wales valleys came from coal mining. A vibrant and remarkably homogeneous society was created. In 1901, seventy per cent of working men were in the collieries, and although the Nonconformist chapels were a strong force in social cohesion, the welfare halls, institutes, parks and libraries that were built and maintained by the miners became increasingly important from the 1880s. By the 1930s there were more than a hundred such arrays of civic amenities serving valleys communities. Gilfach was late in the field. Plans to found a workmen's hall and institute were first laid in 1912 and a library and various educational classes began in adapted premises, but seven years passed before a site for the construction of a hall, close to the bridge that at last linked the two sides of the valley, was purchased for £50 from the landowner, Col. Vaughan Lee, whose manorial home was in Somerset. Building work began and then was abandoned as the money ran out and industrial unrest meant none was coming in. It recommenced in 1923 and the new hall was formally opened in July 1924. My Uncle Will, husband of my father's sister, Julia, a sober-sided character, was secretary of the committee that saw the project through the years of delay to completion, and John Love, my mother's father, conducted the 'Grand Orchestra' throughout the week of celebrations. The Welfare Park, where I played tennis, and table tennis in the pavilion, and rugby, opened in September 1932, just two years before I was born.

Powell Duffryn Associated Collieries, which by a process of amalgamation eventually controlled most of the Gilfach Pits, was based on the company founded by Thomas Powell of Newport. He made a vast fortune from astute exploitation of reserves in the Aberdare valley, and began the export of coal in 1840 with shipments from Cardiff to Nantes. Powell Duffryn was usually known by its initials 'PD'. Stout colliers' boots, supplied, at a price, by the company, were 'PDs'. It was not entirely a laughing matter that employees said the initials stood for 'poverty and death'. From the beginning there was friction between the mine owners, whose sole interest was profit, and the colliers, who worked in unimaginably difficult and dangerous conditions, hundreds of feet below the surface. When the pay was good and steady, the work underground was tolerable, but when owners cut wages, because the price of coal fell, or a pit's output declined, usually for geological reasons beyond control of the men, then the rawness of the relationship burned and occasionally became incandescent.

In 1893, the hauliers went on strike. These were the men who worked the horses hauling filled drams from the coalface to the bottom of the shaft. Three of my Adams great uncles, hauliers in Gilfach at this time, were involved in a dispute that became increasingly acrimonious and violent. The hauliers' chief grievance was the fluctuation in earnings caused by the sliding scale, which linked wages to the market price of coal. This meant that it was in the interests of the owners to sell coal cheaply, and that increased production could be rewarded by wage cuts. A second dispute over the same issue in 1898 resulted in a lockout that lasted six months and brought terrible suffering to the mining communities. The sacrifice, in the end for no gain, engendered greater determination among the men to unite in the stand against the owners. The South Wales Miners' Federation was formed in the same year and shortly afterwards affiliated to the Miners' Federation of Great Britain.

In Gilfach Goch, Joseph Griffiths, whose family had come from Merthyr with Evan Evans, was a leading union activist. After the troubles of 1898, he was barred from working in local collieries, the fate of many who fought on behalf of the miners. With a family to support, he travelled weekly to the anthracite mines in the valleys of south-west Wales, returning home only at weekends. Eventually allowed back, he was joined in the mine by his sons, William, Joseph and Arthur, as each in turn reached the age of thirteen. It was a bookish, Welsh-speaking, chapel-going family, the boys all accomplished musicians. Will, having been for a time a professional violinist in London, became head of the Welsh department of Foyle's bookshop and published books in Welsh under the Gwasg Foyle (Foyle's Press) imprint. There, during the 1930s, he was approached by an unknown writer, Richard Lloyd, who for some time had been trying to write a novel about the south Wales coalfield. Will told him about his father's experiences and introduced him to his family home. The effect on the work in progress was momentous. The author saw how he could shape what threatened to be a sprawling narrative by moulding the story of the Griffiths family into a fiction, taking as much of the history of the 1898 conflict between workers and owners as he wanted, and setting his scene not in the ribbon-like settlements of the Rhondda but in a separate valley, which is recognisably Gilfach. At the end of the novel, the narrator, Huw, is alone remembering his family, all dead or dispersed abroad, and waiting for the first thuds of slag from the encroaching colliery tip against the walls of the home they once shared. This too, is an echo of the history of Gilfach, where a farm, a school and a row of houses were buried under pit waste. The image was so powerful that the book's title was at first *Slag*, but the author thought better of it. When, as Richard Llewellyn, he published it in 1939, it was called *How Green Was My Valley*.

In 1908, D. A. Thomas (later Lord Rhondda), who owned the Cambrian Colliery in Clydach Vale, acquired control of the pits in Penygraig and Llwynypia and then those in Gilfach that had belonged to Archibald Hood and Christmas Evans (the son and heir of Evan Evans) thus forming what became known as the Cambrian Combine. On 1 November 1910, after a period of increasingly acrimonious dispute between the South Wales Miners' Federation and the owners, 27,000 Combine workers in the Rhondda and Gilfach Goch went on strike. They had just grievances: a wage cut of five per cent with the likelihood of further losses due to a new regulation preventing miners from working underground for more than eight hours in twenty-four. The company brought in non-union labour from neighbouring villages by train, which inevitably precipitated a violent response, culminating in what became known as the Tonypandy Riots. The strikers' efforts to prevent these men reaching the pits, and to stop the pumps and so flood the underground workings, were met initially by local police and then by police reinforcements brought in from other regions, including Bristol and London. Finally, the Home Secretary, Winston Churchill, sent in military help at the request of the chief constable of Glamorgan.

No rioting occurred in Gilfach Goch, but there was a similar pattern of protest, with similar consequences. Strikers tried to stop the pumps at the Britannic Colliery and were thought to be planning to roll boulders down the mountain on to the pit. Explosives were stolen and placed by the wall of a manager's house, though there was no explosion. Again, soldiers were summoned. A detachment of Royal Munster Fusiliers was billeted at the school (which they proceeded to rob of its meagre stock) for two months. Fifty Lancashire Fusiliers marched over the mountain through the snow to keep an eye on things, and twenty mounted hussars rode in from Pontypridd and stayed a day at the Glamorgan, the valley's largest hotel. It was an extraordinary example of over-reaction by those in authority. Twelve Gilfach men, charged with violence and intimidation against an under-manager of the Britannic, were brought before the magistrates at Pontypridd on 14 December 1910. Crowds of fellow workers gathered outside the court to protest, but to no purpose. Two of the men were sentenced to twelve months in prison, three were fined, a fourth was bound over. Among the six who were acquitted was William Evans, known as Evans Brawd, a celebrated mountain fighter, who had reformed and, like my grandfather, become a member of the Salvation Army. He claimed he had rescued the under-manager, but that had not saved him from a heavy blow to the head from a police truncheon. You will find a fictionalised portrait of Evans Brawd as the former mountain fighter, Dai Bando, in *How Green Was My Valley*, Huw's protector and boxing tutor. The strike lasted a year and left a legacy of bitterness that the passage of time has hardly dispelled. Notwithstanding his inspirational leadership as prime minister during the Second World War, Winston Churchill's name is still reviled in these parts.

A handful of coal owners and pit managers gained the respect and even the affection of the men. Colliers in Llwynypia contributed substantially to the statue of Archibald Hood that once stood in front of The Library, and David Davies, the agent, was greatly admired. His working life began underground as a twelve year old in 1883 and by educating himself at night classes he had obtained a first-class colliery manager's certificate at the age of twenty-one. In 1896 he moved to Clydach Vale and in less than five years had become manager of the Cambrian No.2 pit. There, in March 1905, he played a leading part in rescuing trapped survivors of an explosion that killed thirty-three men. In the fire that followed the explosion, which extended almost 330 yards along workings fifteen hundred feet underground, the temperature reached 382 degrees centigrade. Extinguishing it took forty days. Water could not be used, and the task was begun by teams of men working in pairs, with only gauntlets and face protection, throwing handfuls of mortar at the flames. My mother's father was a mining contractor with a team of repairmen who may have been working at the Cambrian when the disaster occurred. Certainly about this time he brought his family from Abercarn in Monmouthshire to live in Howard Street, Clydach Vale, overlooking the colliery. Perhaps he was involved in the action following the explosion, and the whole family would have been witnesses of the dreadful aftermath as the dead were brought to their homes in horse-drawn ambulances, and then the funerals. But my mother, who was seven in 1905, never mentioned it. This was not the first and certainly not the last major accident underground, or even at the Cambrian Colliery. In 1965, almost sixty years to the day after the 1905 disaster, Muriel's father was an injured survivor of the explosion there that killed thirty-one of his workmates and friends. He did not work again.

David Davies was one of seven men awarded the Silver Medal of the Royal Humane Society for his part in the 1905 rescue. Early in 1910 he became the agent, that is overall manager, for the group of Combine pits in Gilfach Goch and brought his family to a big house, Bryn Wawr, on the mountain above the terraces on the Evanstown side of the valley. There he remained for the rest of his life, though he actually died suddenly on a walking holiday in Norway in 1931. Davies became fascinated by coal measures fossils, mostly of plants, almost as soon as he began working underground, and by the time he was a pit manager had made himself a considerable expert in the field. He sought to identify the fossils associated with particular coal seams. Because the coal from some seams was valued more highly than that from others, this work was keenly watched by mine owners interested in cross-correlating seams between collieries. Published papers earned him an engraved gold watch from D. A. Thomas, and election as a fellow of the Royal Geological Society. His work brought him friendship with important academic geologists, like Marie Stopes, before she became famous in the field of family planning, and with workers underground, including my grandfather, who contributed to his reference collection of about 16,000 fossil plants now housed in the National Museum of Wales.

***

The troubles in the coalfield did not end with the unrest of 1910. In 1925, unemployment among miners rose to over 28 per cent and it continued to rise. The effects of the depression of the later 1920s and 1930s were particularly severe in Wales because the mines were by far the biggest employers, and because the vast bulk of coal production was for overseas markets that evaporated overnight. In Gilfach Goch, as in the coalfield towns and villages of all the south Wales valleys, miners and their families suffered dreadfully, as the historian, John Davies, from Treorci in the Rhondda Fawr, describes:

In 1926, a family with two children received, at most, one pound a week from the [Poor Law] guardians, but a single man did not get a penny from any public body. Other means of assistance had therefore to be found to save mining communities from starvation. The South Wales Miners' Federation contributed £300,000 to the maintenance of the miners and substantial donations came from workers in the Soviet Union; male-voice choirs went on fund-raising journeys and extensive help was given by those inhabitants of the coalfield who were still in work. Most of the money collected was spent on the soup kitchens, institutions which were of vital importance in the dreary months of 1926. The food they provided was not the only contribution of the soup kitchens: the joint effort they entailed was central to the maintenance of the morale of the community, as were other kinds of communal activity – the jazz bands, for example, and the shoe-repairing centres. But these efforts only scratched the surface of need. By the beginning of the winter of 1926, every mining family was weighed down by debt, many of the children of the coalfield had no shoes and were carried to school on their fathers' backs; the wives, who gave all the available protein to their children and their husbands, were fainting from lack of nourishment; infant mortality was rising rapidly. Under the circumstances, there was no choice but to yield.

I knew nothing of this when I was young. The 1926 strike was never mentioned by my parents, or the parents of my friends, who had lived through it. It was not memorialised in any community activity, although the marching jazz bands had another period of popularity, and a part in inter-village rivalry, in the years immediately following the Second World War. It was not referred to in school. I believe my grandfather, as colliery overman, and my father, as electrician, were among the lucky ones who continued to earn because their work was essential to pit maintenance, but I am not certain, and now it is impossible to find out. They never volunteered information and I did not possess a sense of history well enough developed to ask.

It was only when war with Germany appeared imminent and with it a real threat of disruption to the coal imports on which by this time Britain depended, that the remaining mines (for there had been closures in the long grey years) were geared up to full production and there was work for all. I was almost five: the valley I came to know was busy and the clamour of mining was in our ears day and night.

Two

I DON'T KNOW how old I was when I learned that the first owner of the house where I was born was 'the blind Vicar', and had not thought of enquiring further. Then, sometime in the early 1990s, browsing the autobiography of (Lord) David Owen at George's bookshop in Bristol, I was startled to find a reference to Gilfach Goch: his grandfather was 'the blind Vicar', or curate rather, a distinction evidently lost on those at home who had spoken of him. A little research revealed his name, George Morgan Llewellyn, and background. He was the son of William Llewellyn, who had made a fortune as grocer and provision merchant in the neighbouring Ogmore valley. The grand Gwalia grocery shop, now in the National History Museum at St Fagans, was the family business.

Much of what I know of the history of the house and how it came into the possession of my grandfather, a miner, is owed to family documents that survived by the merest chance. My bedroom as a child had a diminutive fake-Georgian window to the front, its ten small panes affording a cluttered view of a slice of the valley, though at first I should have needed to stand on a chair to see out of it. A larger sash window to the side overlooked the neighbour's back yard. Apart from the iron-framed single bed and a wooden chair, the only piece of furniture in the room was a typical bow-fronted Victorian chest of drawers. The drawer on the right at the top was full of papers, which I would turn over from time to time looking for any that had meaning, but beyond birth and marriage certificates none did. When my sisters and I cleared the house after our father died, I could tell no one else had bothered to look at the contents in decades. My youthful rummaging had left them in a disordered jumble and, as there was no time for sorting and reflection, I transferred them into a couple of plastic bags, which I stowed in the loft here for more than thirty years. It was only when the need to find out more about my family became urgent and I was prepared to consider anything, that I emptied the bags and began properly to look. Then, what surprises!

One of the papers, a formal solicitor's notice, revealed that in December 1912 the Reverend George Llewellyn acquired the lease of a parcel of land, part of the Lanelay Estate, from the landowner, Arthur Vaughan Hanning Vaughan-Lee Esq., of Dillington Park in Somerset, and presumably The Parsonage was built soon afterwards. By 1916, however, Llewellyn had been appointed to the living of Llandow, near Cowbridge, where he spent the rest of his life. The same document noted that on 18 August 1916 the lease was assigned to Samuel Adams, my grandfather, described as Colliery Overman, subject to the payment of a yearly ground rent of £3 14s. He renamed the house The Cottage, and for many years an embossed copper nameplate to that effect, tarnished almost beyond legibility, though you could still feel the raised cursive letters, was attached to the outer wall of the porch.

I was left to puzzle where a colliery worker could raise the funds to make such a purchase. Burrowing through the layers of documents sometime later, I came upon two small sheets of unlined notepaper bearing the address 'Gorwyl, Ogmore Vale, Glam.' – the home of William Llewellyn, the affluent grocer. The first showed that on 19 August 1916 my grandfather entered into a mortgage agreement with William Llewellyn for the sum of £240, and that on 20 February 1917 a payment of £86 had reduced the debt to £160, interest of £6 having been added in the half-year. By 31 July 1918 the outstanding debt had reduced to £147 (including a further £7 interest), when it was paid in full.

I like to think my grandfather was entirely trustworthy, but what confidence did William Llewellyn have in him as a business proposition? Census returns suggest an explanation:

he was probably already acquainted with Samuel Adams, and his parents, because in 1871 they lived at Tynewydd Road, Ogmore Vale, while the Llewellyn family and servants occupied three adjoining properties in Tynewydd Street nearby. The Gwalia Stores opened in the same or adjacent premises in 1880, no more than a hundred yards from my great-grandparents' home. At this point documentary evidence runs out and conjecture begins. It occurred to me that the choice of Gilfach Goch as the Reverend Llewellyn's first parish was perhaps influenced by knowledge that there was a family in the village on whom he could rely for help if the need arose.

As a child and while growing up, I thought of the house as ours, my parents', my sisters' and mine. It was only much later that I saw it was really the home made by my father's mother and father. It had come to us because Dats, my grandfather, who must have held me newly born, but whom, with unfocused infant eyes, I had never properly seen, bought it in 1916, and because Mam, my grandmother, willed it.

***

I was just three when I first had the idea of tagging along behind a group of children passing the house on their way to school. They drew me from our front garden, past the corner and the familiar shops, over the bridge with its fantastic superstructure of criss-crossing steel bars, where railway engines hauling coal wagons ran underneath, gushing clouds of white smoky vapour through rusted gaps at the foot of the corrugated sheets that stopped you falling onto the track, up the hill called Coronation Road and another short, steeper pitch to the schools, infants' and girls' one side, boys' the other. I came home dinnertime, with the other children, saying, 'I'm not going there again. They make you lie down like a lot of bloody cows.' I can see now the long, low tables at which the youngest children sat in little tub armchairs, and the pillows that, twice daily, were placed on the tables for us to lay our heads on, close our eyes and pretend to sleep.

My mother and sisters repeated this story from time to time, but no one ever mentioned any concern about my disappearance early one day when I was three. Perhaps they guessed what had happened. Perhaps, when they enquired, neighbours said, 'I saw him going off to school with the other boys.' Children were not taken to school in those days; they went unaccompanied. Communication between school and parents was very rare. If there had been some alarm in the infants' classroom at the unexpected arrival of a new pupil, which seems doubtful, it would not have been easy for teachers to get in touch with my mother, for we had no telephone, even if the school did, which I think unlikely. My adventure seems to have been received coolly on all sides. At home, what was remembered was my determination, with an epithet learned from my cousin Bloom, not to go back to school, though of course I did when I was four.

That would have been in 1939. The macadamised road stopped short at the end of Kenry Street, after which it continued unmade and rough. Within twenty yards it crossed over a brook, piped beneath, and just beyond, to the right, was a gated entrance and short flight of steps, walled on either side, to the yard of the boys' school. Thirty yards farther, on the left, the rubble strewn track reached the entrance to the infants' and the girls' school, which shared that site. The school buildings were like scores of others up and down the valleys, built about the turn of the nineteenth century – and built to last – of local dark grey stone with redbrick trimming for windows and doors. Behind a high stone wall, the asphalt play yard of the infants' sloped gently to a lean-to lavatory block and stinking boys' urinal. At the top of the yard, underneath the classrooms, through high arched openings that would not have been out of place in a church or priory, were shelters for play when it was too wet, windy or cold to run about in the open. The floor was of stone flags and there was a narrow bench along the whitewashed walls, but the shelters were unlit and had rather mysterious dark corners. They were a place for secrets: there I discovered how girls differed from boys. The classrooms had tall, many-paned windows set so high in the wall no child could possibly see out of them and most adults only by standing on a chair. Below the windows, a shining, brown-tiled dado descended to a woodblock floor, unstained and never polished, so far as one could tell, the colour of old, dirty straw.

After the youngest infants' class we sat in twos in iron-framed, wooden desks. Miss Jones wore boldly floral smocks over her everyday clothes, and spectacles. She was motherly and had greying dark, curly hair, and spoke in a plaintive contralto. Lacking the disposition to be irritated or angered at our behaviour, she seemed rather puzzled by it, and hurt. Charts with faded illustrations hung around the walls announcing the letters of the alphabet, which we recited chorally as she pointed to each in turn – 'ah for apple … buh for ball …'. Perhaps there were reading books, and we must have practised writing and learned our numbers.

After Miss Jones's class, boys and girls separated. The girls moved up to the adjacent girls' school building while we crossed the road to the boys' school, where to begin with there was another Miss Jones, younger but already matronly, who was even more baffled by the unruly element among us. Quite soon she married small, thickset Mr Saunders, a craft teacher for the oldest boys. One of his highly polished brown boots had a thick sole and he walked with a stick and a heavy limp.

As well as silver-painted iron pipes and radiators, I remember the fireplaces near the door in the boys' school classrooms, and the fires that burned in them when the weather was particularly cold, and the bucket of coals in the hearth. There was a blackboard on the wall at the front of the class and a big board on an easel to one side. A pale, thin cane hung by its crook over the wooden frame of the blackboard on the wall, behind the imposing teacher's desk on stout wooden runners. Mr David came to the school when I was eight, and my recall of events sharpens with his arrival. He was a young man, black-haired, beetle-browed, bespectacled and pale, with sunken cheeks. His Welsh accent was not one we were familiar with, and from time to time he cleared his throat, a prolonged grating rattle, spat a heavy gob on the woodblock floor and rubbed the mess in with the sole of his shoe. Though spitting, outdoors, was not unusual where men's lungs were clogged with coal dust, the first time this occurred we were stunned. Soon, even the roughest of my companions were disgusted. He became known to us as Gawker, though goodness knows who coined the name or what we thought it meant.

Gawker couldn't teach, couldn't keep order. When the noise of unrestrained conversations, shouting across the class, shuffling feet, scuffles between pupils, became more than he could bear, he would seize the cane and call out a boy, more or less at random, and slash the palm and fingers of his open hand. We watched this performance in silence, but once the victim had returned to his seat, shaking the stinging hand and then thrusting it in an armpit and wincing, the noise would start again – and continue until the next boy was ordered to the front. The whole day passed in this mode. Some work was done. This I recall because I see myself trying to hide what I had written from Billy Woods, the boy placed next to me, who was intent on copying it, and in the end usually succeeded. As I dipped into the desk inkwell and scratched with my school pen, I would shield my book with my left arm, while he peered over or under my elbow.

I was a docile, watchful child, younger and smaller than the rest, and the punishment lot fell to me only once, but Billy was often caned. At playtime one morning, when we should all have been in the yard, Billy, whose dirt- and ink-stained hand had already been stung that day, sneaked into the empty classroom, took the cane and broke it. The cane was an official instrument, perhaps not readily replaced, or perhaps Gawker, for shame's sake, did not want to admit his had disappeared and ask for another. The rest of the day he struggled on, deprived of the means of obtaining even a momentary pause in the hullabaloo, and the next morning appeared with two thicker sticks, without crooks – found, made or bought outside. With these he laid about him fairly freely to maintain some sort of grip on events in the class – and some days or weeks later, Billy, whose earlier act of rebellion had gone undetected, slipped into the classroom at playtime and made away with both.

A rational adult would have sought some other solution at that point. Gawker came to school the next day with a bundle of rods like the fasces symbol that often figured with Mussolini in wartime cartoons (though without the axe), and the battle of wills continued. About this time older class members, released at the end of afternoon school, would stage an ambush. Scooping up stones from the side of the brook as they went, they hastened across the rough, open ground to the corner of the back lane between the gardens of Kenry Street and Wyndham Street where they could watch without being seen. As Gawker emerged from the school gate they hurled stones at him and he ran for the shelter of the terraced houses. Anarchy spread through the class until everyone joined in and stones arced after the fleeing figure in a dense shower. I do not know how long this continued, but at one point our class teacher waited until other members of staff were ready to leave and they came down the canyon of steps and out of the gate together, and stones followed all of them as they ran for cover.

In my recollection, the events I have described seem to have followed quickly one upon the other, and I don't know now whether they occurred in the course of a term, or half a term – or a whole year. My memory tells me only that, quite suddenly, Mr David is no longer there. And what of him? I think he may well have died young. What I see now is a sick man (if he had been fit, he would have been in the forces), who suffered from a chronic chest complaint, and lacked the strength and energy to teach, or certainly to teach thirty-five or more boys, most with nothing before them in a very few years, but a tramp to the pit with their fathers.

Badly taught as we had been, and without prospect of continuing in school beyond leaving age (then fourteen), would that have been my destiny? And would it have been a bad thing to grow closer to my father as I shared his experience of the pit? Would his talent with machines have rubbed off on me? Would we have spent our leisure together maintaining his motorbike, or *our* motorbikes? Gone to the Con Club in the evening for a pint and a chat, a game of solo perhaps, with friends who worked with us in the Squint? I loved and respected him and regret our lives diverged: we had so little in common, so little to exchange, one with another, in the inconsequential quotidian ways of father and son.

It might, then, have been different; but our new teacher, Mr Williams, was competent, well organised, in control of the disparate elements in the class pulling this way and that. There were still occasional moments of high drama, as on the day when Georgie Morgan was called out to be caned. What he did to deserve punishment I have no idea, but what followed I shall not forget. Georgie was one of the older boys, thin and of exceptional pallor, with pale hair that stood up at angles over his narrow skull. He rose slowly from his place, with the look of one unjustly accused, dragged his feet as he came to the teacher's desk in front of the class and held out his hand reluctantly. A fraction of a second before the cane struck, he withdrew it and took a backward step. 'Hold out your hand.' The cane was raised and descended rather more sharply, but again the hand was withdrawn and another step backwards took pupil and teacher, now red in the face, further across the room. A third swish of the cane produced the same result and a step to the rear brought Georgie close to the blackboard and easel, which he dodged around and made for the classroom door. As he ran down the corridor we heard his shout, 'I'll tell my father about you.' In the silence that followed we looked at one another, eyes wide: Georgie's father was Freddie Morgan, former bantamweight champion. Nothing came of it, of course. Parents didn't go to schools in those days.

Smart, vigorous, with dark hair and moustache beginning to grey, Mr Williams, 'Eddie', was not a man to be trifled with. He had keen eyes and reacted quickly to lapses in behaviour or effort. He also examined our work with care, showed us where we had gone wrong and helped us understand better how to put things right, in arithmetic and English, the essential elements of the school day. But there was more to him: he enjoyed using the blackboard artistically and had a good voice and a love of drama. The best of every week was Friday afternoon, when he read poems to us from a battered book that had survived from some gas-lit Edwardian parlour. We soon knew our favourites and asked for them again and again – 'Bishop Hatto', 'The Inchcape Rock', 'After Blenheim', 'Sohrab and Rustum', 'Little Billee', 'The Destruction of Sennacherib' – until we could have joined in the recitation, and some we remember still. He wrote on the blackboard for us to copy I Corinthians 13, 'Though I speak with the tongues of men and of angels', the Authorised Version, and we learned it. At the end of the year, four of us had passed the 'scholarship', the examination for entry to the grammar school in Tonyrefail.

***

I began properly to learn about things outside home and near neighbours and shops as the war began in 1939. I was across the road in the house of Mr and Mrs Vaughan and their five children, all of them boys, when the announcement of the declaration of war came on the wireless. I know now it was 11 o'clock on Sunday morning, 3 September. For those broadcast minutes everyone was quiet, and we listened. What it would mean I had no idea, but something about the occasion, I suppose the reaction of others, imprinted it on my memory. The two older Vaughan boys, Douglas and Glyn, soon joined the forces, Billy worked in the pit; George and the youngest, Trevor, already in the elementary school, were my friends. My wider explorations of Gilfach Goch and the mountains that rose about it were made in their company.

By the time I became aware of things beyond our doors, the threat of war had brought increased demand for coal and there was work for every able-bodied man, and soon even for some women, who, like my sister Joan, travelled daily by train to a munitions factory in Bridgend. The Gilfach of my boyhood was busy and noisy. You cannot live close to a pit, as most of us did, without being aware of it. After hooters calling the men to work, in early morning darkness came the crunch of steel-shod boots on the road, followed soon after by the percussion of steam engines, the creaking and clatter of moving trucks and drams, the grating roar of tipped slag and countless unaccountable thuds and clanks that continued all through the day and, during the winter, deep into darkness once more. So all-pervading was the noise that we did not notice it. A sudden silence would have been startling.

Across the road, at the bottom of the Vaughans' garden, not fifty yards from our front door, was an unfenced drop of about fifteen feet to the railway lines that carried the long, long trains of black wagons empty up the valley and heaped with coal down. On the far side of the double track was the incline along which 'journeys' of drams were hauled loaded with coal from the pit, and the screens, a structure of corrugated sheets within which a moving belt carried the contents of dramload after dramload. There, surface workers separated the coal, large and small, from slag, which was tipped on the further side of the incline where it crashed and tumbled down into the black river, the Ogwr Fach. Our house was so close to the colliery that, if he were working on the surface, my father would come home for his snack at 11 o'clock in the morning. The kettle was always singing on the hob to make his black tea, and bread and cheese were ready, just in case. I see him still, hanging up the flat cap he always wore to work and sitting at the table in his pit-clothes, his face smirched with coal dust.

Often in the hazy march between waking and sleeping, I go back to the house. I open the front gate and close it behind, listening for that peculiar clink of the latch, and walk up the curving path through the porch to the big front door with its gleaming brass knocker, which Tim, our black and white tomcat, would reach up to and knock as firmly as any human, and I am home. Or I hover wraith-like by the walls, gazing in through windows. My mother is sitting in the kitchen corner, her poor wasted legs close to the fire, my father, his white hair slicked back from the bath, is in an armchair in the back room, feet up, newspaper spread across his chest, eyes closed; while my sister Barbara dusts the mirrored sideboard in the front room with swift, vigorous rubs, setting the ornate drawer handles rattling.

Our house stood on its own, atop a little hill of front lawn, separated from its neighbours by narrow gullies. The gate with its distinctive clink was not as tall and barbarously spiked as those of our neighbours, almost all of which hung at an angle from their hinges and ground grimly on the stone threshold as you struggled them open. The bars of our gate were slim and arched at the top and it swung easily between tall pillars of red brick with solid red pyramidal finials. From the gate, a redbrick wall ran the width of the property, gradually diminishing in height to another, shorter pillar. This was similarly capped, so that the wall and the low fence, its bars arched like the gate set into it, were horizontal against the gradient of the road beyond.

Most of the village shops were close by, gathered around a T-junction, where High Street, the long road beginning just below our house and extending to the top of the valley, was met at right angles and at the top of a gentle slope by the road from Evanstown, which we took each day to school. Facing this junction, the top-piece of the 'T', was a grand Co-op, which had departments for hardware and footwear, general groceries and meat, and on the other side of the road, men's and women's clothes (made to measure if required), and a dispensing chemist. On one of the street corners opposite the Co-op were the windows of Griffiths's Bon Marché, crowded with dresses and blouses, scarves and hats and coats, and on the other was Joe Bacchetta's, the most frequented of all Gilfach's shops.

Joe and dumpling plump 'Mrs' sold cigarettes and tobacco, sweets and chocolates, pop and ice cream. They had a son, Johnny (Giovanni, or Gianni, I suppose) and a daughter, Doreen, both of whom shared the family commitment to the business. On cold days, when the little stove in the middle of the shop floor was lit, you would find idlers perched on the high-backed, fawn plywood benches, pierced with a million round holes, which ran around the walls, sipping hot Oxo from elaborately shaped and decorated Oxo cups. Our Italian corner shops did not have coffee machines. When the war came, Joe, like Luigi Tambini and Johnny Rabaiotti, was interned on the Isle of Man. It is hard to imagine a trio less capable of sabotage and treachery. Young Johnny, barely in his teens, took over the running of the shop with his mother and immediately lost his boyishness. It was he who sold slices of swiss roll at tuppence each and doubled the profit on one wrapped cake. The return of the internees to their shops on the conclusion of hostilities was greeted with almost as much pleasure as the return of ice cream.

Tambini's fish and chip shop was up the road next to the Co-op chemists. There, another capable 'Mrs' carried on the business while her husband languished in internment. She had a teenage daughter, Carrie, to help her, but I don't remember her sons in the shop. Val, the youngest, born a few days after me, was a friend and we sometimes played together in his back garden. He showed me the cellar where potatoes were stored, and washed and peeled. Once I climbed a rusty fence there to retrieve a ball and clambered back, and it was only when Val asked what I had done to my hand that I saw I had pierced

41

my palm on a spike and that it bled profusely but – until that moment of realisation – painlessly. His mother held my hand under streaming cold water and carefully pressed flaps of skin back together and bound a clean rag around my palm. And it healed, leaving a fine, curving white scar that seems to have vanished now, though for many years it was still visible.

Beyond Tambini's was Spearing's, a gloomy little delicatessen, where, most Wednesdays, we bought Palethorpe's pork pies to have warmed for lunch. A little further up the road, next door to my Aunty Sarah's, was a greengrocer, a little further again, Jefferies the newsagent's and, at the end of the terrace, Johnny Rabaiotti's Italian corner shop, except that it wasn't quite on the corner. Beyond that, a broad and steep dirt track led down to The Globe, Dai Griffiths's fleapit cinema, which had threepenny benches down at the front underneath the screen. Shows there could be unpredictable, because before entering the projection box Dai had usually taken a pint or two at the Glamorgan Hotel. It was not unknown for reels of film to be run in the wrong order, and resolution of the plot revealed before the complexities of character and action that should have led up to it. Far more frequently voice and action slowed dramatically a moment or two before the film broke and the screen blared white. A cacophony of catcalls and stamping on bare floorboards would follow while someone up in the box struggled with fuddled fingers to splice the broken ends of film. Eleven such interruptions occurred during a presentation of Laurence Olivier's *Henry V*, which in consequence went on an hour beyond the scheduled time.

A diagonal route of twenty yards across the road from our front garden would bring you to the steps of the Con Club, men only, which was always packed on Sundays, because the law then forbade the opening of pubs on the Sabbath. Next to the Con was the post office, and then Pegler's grocery, which greeted you with a faintly resinous scent of fresh sawdust liberally spread on the floor. To the right, under a grey and white marble-topped counter, a rank of tilted biscuit tins revealed their contents under glazed covers, while above, a majestic red and gleaming steel man-powered machine sliced bacon and cold meats to the thickness of your choice. To the left, behind a red mahogany counter, shelves sparsely stacked with dry goods reached to the ceiling. A few deep, open shelves for vegetables occupied a corner at the end of the mahogany counter. Once, when I was very young, I was sent to Pegler's to buy potatoes and asked for three pounds. The woman behind the counter appraised me with lifted eyebrows.

'Three pounds?'

'Yes.' She reached for a smaller bag.

'They won't go far,' said my mother. 'What did you ask for?'

'Three pounds of potatoes.'

'Ah,' she said, 'it was three pennyworth we wanted.'

There were no recriminations, but it was acutely embarrassing: I had been foolish, and everyone knew. It was a long time before I could be persuaded to go again on an errand to Pegler's, and I have never forgotten the experience.

Before I started school, this section of High Street with its busy shops was the limit of my known world, where I walked, as I well remember, holding the hand of Mam, my grandmother. And it was she, I feel sure, who first introduced me to those of our neighbours whom I would greet by name. Opposite our house, next door to the Vaughans lived Mrs Jones, a widow, whose husband, Tom, I barely remember, but know he was a haulier in the Squint, and that he died in his forties from Weil's disease – the consequence of working always near horse fodder and, inevitably, rats, in a wet mine. George Murphy, the postman, lived next to Mrs Jones's. No doubt he had a wife and family, who have left no trace on my memory, but him I remember well, Punch-faced, with a wide and wicked toothless grin beneath his hard-peaked post office cap. A few doors further down, the last house in the row belonged to Mr and Mrs Parry, whose daughter, Megan, married my cousin Bloom. They had a greenhouse on their large corner plot; Bill Parry was a keen gardener. My father seemed not to trust him, I shall never now know why, and notwithstanding our love for Bloom, we had no contact with them.

Old Mr and Mrs Lester lived next door to us, and next to them was bent and aged Mrs Driscoll, whom we saw daily making her faltering way across the back lane to a rickety chicken cot. Her few hens were imprisoned in a small yard surrounded by a high stake fence, brittle and green with mould, which they might easily have pushed down had they possessed the instinct to escape. The conscription of younger men to fight brought change to both houses. Mrs Driscoll's married daughter, small and fair-haired, returned to the safety of home with her son Malcolm, and the Lesters' daughter-in-law, Olwen, came to them with her son David, who soon became my friend Dai. Malcolm, who was little more than a baby when he arrived in Gilfach, I came to know later as a fellow chorister at the mission church.

Fred Brown and his wife lived next door to Mrs Driscoll. Fred, who worked in the Squint, had the tough and swarthy look of a gipsy about him, whereas Mrs Brown was round-faced and pale. He was wiry, while she appeared plump, though that might have been at least partly due to the superabundance of clothing she habitually wore. Outdoors, whatever the weather, she would face the world in a long gabardine coat, green with age, a beret pulled down to her ears, and a dark plaid shawl over her shoulders and tied about her neck. She wore the shawl indoors, as I saw when I called at their house from time to time. They let their front room to Morgan the dentist, from Tonypandy, who, with a stark minimum of equipment and care, pulled teeth on Sunday afternoons. Conventional wisdom of the time said it was better to have all your teeth out, good or bad, and a full false set fitted, thereby guaranteeing no further dental problems. Morgan, a dentist of the old school, concurred with this; the idea of saving a tooth never crossed his mind. The Browns' house harboured a distinctive odour of Friar's Balsam that suggested Mrs Brown frequently hoisted the shawl from her shoulders over her head to inhale a steaming lungful of the pungent mixture. I knew this penetrating odour was unconnected with Morgan's dubious practice because I had other reasons for visiting. The Browns had an attractive busty daughter with long blond hair falling about her shoulders, the film star look of the time, who worked in Barry, perhaps the docks, in daily contact with American servicemen. Some weekends she brought home big packs of Camels or Lucky Strikes, each containing two hundred cigarettes, which non-smoking GIs obtained very cheaply at the PX to trade with civilians. Whenever the glamorous daughter was seen on the road, I would be dispatched to the aromatic fug of the Brown's with hopeful coins. What the daughter paid or traded for the cigarettes no one paused to think.

The last house in the street, where the Reverend George Llewellyn, 'the blind vicar', had lived when he first came to Gilfach, was the home of the Protheroes. They had built a garage next to the house, but beyond that was a gap of about a hundred yards along which the pavement was bordered by a stout retaining wall holding back creeping soil and the steep grey tip from Lock's abandoned mine. Then came one of Gilfach's dozen pubs, the Gilfach Hotel, which was kept by Uncle Reg and Aunty Bernice, my mother's sister. The Protheroes had two daughters. Beryl, pale, freckled and serious, her dark hair in plaits, was about my age and occasionally, when I was ten or eleven, I played hop-scotch on the pavement by the pub with Beryl and my cousins, Molly and Merell, twin blonde daughters of my aunt and uncle, who were a few years younger. There were not many children in our section of High Street: George and Trevor, before the war brought Dai to join us, and Beryl. It was a settled part of the valley, where most families were mature, their offspring grown up and in many cases already living elsewhere.

It was only when I climbed the mountain with George and

Trevor that I began to comprehend the valley. The road that passed our house carried on up to its top, where it swung around the Trane colliery and its attendant slag heaps, crossed the river and passed between Gilfach's third working pit, the Britannic, and an alpine range of tips, as (now Abercerdin Road) it started down the other side towards a large chapel and a small cluster of shops at a crossroads. There, if you turned left, you found yourself at the top of a straight, steep hill, Coronation Road, lined both sides by terraced houses. At the bottom the road continued straight and unnaturally flat along the top of another tip made of waste from the Squint, which, long before, had included still glowing ashes from the engine house. It proved a combustible mix and during my elementary schooldays wisps of smoke, which stank sulphurously in wet weather, began to rise from long fissures in the tarmac of road and pavement. This volcanic zone terminated at the bridge with its prominent steel super-structure painted battleship grey, and the road went on, past the Workmen's Hall, to close the loop at the T-junction with its cluster of shops fifty or so yards above our house.

At the foot of the smouldering tip the river ran through a cylindrical brick-built culvert, ochre and orange where the water ran, with a tide-mark edge of green slime. In the summer, when the water was low, I watched older boys with longer legs traverse this slightly sloping dank tube by zigzag leaping from side to side. Once started it was impossible to stop before a final, longer jump propelled a distant jagged figure, silhouetted momentarily in the circle of daylight, out of sight and onto the slag-strewn bank at the other end. I tried it once myself before I left the elementary school, my feet landing nearer and nearer the water as I progressed until I slipped and sat in the stream to slide helplessly into the pool gouged at the exit.

In the second phase of my childhood explorations I learned that, down the hill from our house, the road stretched out beyond the Gilfach Hotel, past a redbrick urinal on the left and the railway station on the right. There were no passenger trains, apart from rare summer specials to Porthcawl and, during the war years, the daily service for Bridgend ordnance factory workers. Coal and, occasionally, goods' wagons were the station's staple fare. A broad path of ginger-stained boards crossed the lines and beyond the fence on the other side was the Squint office. A steep, rubble-covered path curved away from the office to the colliery, a drift mine, which was almost at the bottom of the valley. The uncontrolled railway crossing was a route to work for miners and a convenient all-purpose shortcut that I often used.

Beyond the urinal was a gap in which the mountain sloped steeply to a low wall that stopped it tumbling onto the pavement. Then came a row of houses known as Gelliarael Road. The second or third house, set back a little, was the sweet shop where Lyndon Price lived, probably the closest friend of my grammar school years. Eventually we went up to Aberystwyth together with the express purpose of studying geography, though in the end neither of us carried on to honours. At the end of Gelliarael Road the largest of the valley's quarries had been hacked out of the mountain. Although easily accessible, I do not recall seeing anyone play there or attempt to climb its almost vertical curving wall of red rocks and clay.

The quarry occupied a zone we might have considered no-man's-land, for beyond was 'the City'. Its children went to a different school and belonged to a different tribe. The intense rivalry between us reached a climax one Saturday in the summer of 1944, when battle lines were drawn up on the mountain above our house, and Top kids and City kids hurled stones at one another. I watched charge and counter charge from the patch of grass at the back of the house where I lay on a deckchair with my left leg in a plaster cast, having fallen from a tree and torn an ankle ligament a few days earlier. Here and there, stones thrown in skirmishes on the edge of the battlefield fell close to houses and in the road. Clearly something had to be done. The following Monday every boy in the upper classes of the valley's three elementary schools was caned, including some who, with justification, pleaded innocence.

It should not have been a surprise that boys from different parts of the valley formed gangs and that gangs occasionally made alliances that transformed random bickering into large-scale fights. It was the war, of course, the real war, that inspired and possessed us. The war was in every wireless news bulletin, every daily paper, every cinema newsreel. For a time we carried gas masks wherever we went, and took coupons from our ration books to buy sweets. The school windows were crossed with tape to hold the arrowing shards that would shred us if a bomb fell nearby.

And there was a bomb once. It fell out of the blackness of night a few days before Christmas 1940, jettisoned by a raider trying to find its way back to an airfield in occupied northern France. Although I had previously thought this stray was heading home from an attack elsewhere in Wales, I now believe that it was returning from the terrible blitz on Liverpool, where, between 20 and 22 December, 365 people were killed. We were lucky: the bomb landed on the lower slope of the mountain just behind the church. Our house was only a few hundred yards away, but the explosion, muffled perhaps by the boggy terrain where it fell, did not disturb my sleep. I was told about it at breakfast and soon joined others walking purposefully up Glamorgan Terrace and along the dirt road at the back of High Street towards the church. In the gloom of the winter morning a small crowd on the hillside marked the site. They were gathered around a deep crater fully thirty feet across, a cone of brown mud sunk into the ground and still smoking, like an inverted volcano. Here and there in the excavated pile of mud thrown up at the rim were bits of shrapnel from the bomb case, jagged chunks of metal, like lightning crystallised, four or five inches long and heavy in the hand. These, suddenly desirable, were hunted in the red clay and when found, still hot from the explosion, brandished triumphantly.

In the rush to view the crater, I had passed the doctor's house and surgery without taking in the more spectacular damage that had occurred there. Plainer daylight revealed the roof and first floor of what had been a handsome detached house – slates, bricks, broken window frames and splintered rafters, beds, dressing tables and wardrobes – heaped within the ground floor walls and tumbled in the front garden. Furniture, light-fittings, household goods, floral wallpaper were all embarrassingly revealed. I was almost ashamed to look. The back wall of the property abutted the dirt road and there a cellar door had been blown open. Peering in, we could see, among shattered glass and debris, the doctor's store of medical stuff and great jars, tawny brown and blue. It was all strange, part of a familiar, settled world shaken and displaced. The doctor and his wife, dug out of the wreckage and taken to hospital, survived. The war had come to us out of the night and no one had been killed.

We soon became accustomed to the change. The roof of the church, which appeared undamaged, had been lifted bodily by the blast and shifted dangerously. The church was closed; it was not repaired and re-opened for twenty years. The doctor's house remained a ruined pile until after the war, when the site was cleared. I don't know now whether it was destroyed by a second, smaller bomb or by some freak blast from the one that fell on the mountain. For a week or so shards of bomb collected from the crater could be swopped for foreign stamps or cigarette cards. The two I gouged from the mud were displayed on the kitchen windowsill where they rusted through the war years and eventually disappeared, along with other fragmentary mementoes – a stylised eagle with wings spread, a wreathed swastika in its talons, the badge, yellow on green, of a Nazi flyer, the rectangular chrome handgrip I believed was from a parachute, two or three British cap badges, a few brass cartridge cases. I don't regret their loss.

49

We in George Vaughan's gang regularly engaged in what he called 'commando training' – running, leaping brooks, clambering up quarries and throwing stones at targets, for which the remains of a colliery engine house, less than fifty yards from our back gate, was the perfect place. In a theatrical hollow created by tips of grey shale on three sides, two parallel broken walls, about fifteen feet apart and mostly three or four feet in height with stout iron reinforcements protruding, were all that remained of the building. Between the stunted walls was a huge, iron winding wheel, leaning back on its axle, with room enough for a child to crouch inside and imagine himself within a machine, plane, tank or submarine, and so long as he did not inopportunely wriggle out, safe from missiles. The top of the tips surrounding these relics was a flat narrow plain, one fenced corner of which was occupied by Tom Moss's tar-blackened chicken cots. Beyond the fence a higher tip, overlooking the road, the railway station and the Squint, fell steeply almost to the wall of the unkempt garden of Aunty Bernice and Uncle Reg's pub, the Gilfach.

A brook, which had its source at a spring line high on the steep hillside, wound across the flattened top of the tip and tumbled down into the hollow making a sticky bog to one side of the wrecked engine house where rushes grew abundantly. And beyond the rushes, where the tip was lower, was a rusted iron dram, its wheels sunk beyond movement in the shale under its thin veneer of soil and sparse grass. This magical place was called Lock's, and the pond where the brook reached the tip was Lock's Pond, a small, shallow pool fringed on the mountain side by another boggy zone of tall rushes, the abode of frogs and newts. A time would arrive each spring when the pond would be thick with transparent speckled jelly. Lame Tom Moss maintained the pond, repairing occasional breaches in its low wall of stones and turfs (which we called 'clodgins') because he needed the water for his fowls. Much later I discovered that Lock's owed its familiar name to a small coal owner, James Lock, who worked a level on the hillside not far from where we played. In 1911, a miner and his fourteen-year-old son were drowned there. In its healing way the earth had begun to cover up the site of this tragedy, but it was still visible when we were young, a place to avoid among the tall bracken: behind the bricked-up arch slowly being swallowed by the mountain another great flood might be biding its time.

Neighbours in High Street occasionally dumped buckets of ashes and household rubbish just beyond the patch of rushes in the dip, close to the broken walls. This communal midden was favoured by Tom Moss's chickens, which came clucking down the tip to scratch nests in the ashes and roost. It also supplied us with all the tin cans and bottles we could wish for target practice. We spent hours hurling stones from the top of the tip at pillars of rusted cans and bottles on the walls and jars upended on the iron bars that ran through them. I knew this perfect playground from infancy, because my father's big black shed was there, its wide doors facing the iron wheel, about a dozen yards off. Built of corrugated sheets, the shed had also been part of the colliery, perhaps the stables. My father kept his motorbike there.

My friends George and his younger brother, Trevor, were the sons of Sid Vaughan, the Co-op butcher. They lived in Etna Terrace, a row of grey, pebble-dashed semi-detached houses across the road from us, named after the coal company that bought James Lock's lease on the mineral rights in our part of the valley. They were older, George by five years and Trevor three, and so far ahead of me in school I have no recollection of them in classroom or playground. I wonder now whether I was thought a nuisance, calling on them as often as I did, but I was never excluded, so far as I was aware. Their kitchen and living room, and the lavatory with its broad box-like wooden seat and hole in the middle, next to the coalhouse and a step from the back door, were familiar to me. Mrs Vaughan, pale, anxious and quiet, overworked by her all-male family, didn't seem to mind my presence, and I

51

avoided her husband, a blusterer whose customary tone of voice was a snarl.

Ours was, in any case, largely an out-of-doors friendship. Their garden, with the railway line running at the bottom, afforded a small, uneven patch of grass near the house where a tent could be pitched and on warm days in settled weather we read and exchanged comics in the tent; George and Trevor had *Hotspur* and *Rover*, I brought *Wizard*. George was interested in science. From time to time he would bring out a hand-cranked electrical generator from which dangled two terminals. While Trevor or I held the terminals in our palms, he would crank the generator until we had a stinging shock and dropped them with a howl. Or he might persuade Trevor and, if he were there, Dai Lester, to take a terminal each while I completed the circle by holding their other hands, then as George cranked the handle furiously, we three danced to the tingle of electricity. He meddled with electrical fittings in the house until his mother became afraid to turn on switches and even the tap over the sink. At that point his father stepped in. It was an experiment with petrol that nearly undid him. On one of our rambles we found a petrol can and brought it back to the garden in Etna Terrace. There was no witness to what we were doing, unless the beans on their poles and the potato rows were watching tremulously. George shook the can: there was no sound of liquid. He took off the cap and held it upside-down: not a drop emerged. He looked into it (still nothing), and took a box of matches from his pocket, lit one and dropped it into the dark interior. There was an almighty thump and the can, George and the rest of us sprang in different directions. When we recovered ourselves, we could see the can, some distance off, had been ruptured by the force of the explosion and George looked pale beneath his freckles and oddly different. He had lost his eyebrows and the sandy hair that hung over his forehead. At length the hair grew again, with a slight curl it hadn't possessed before, and the eyebrows returned. It could have been worse.

We often wandered the riverbank down the *cwm*. Although filthy, the Ogwr Fach still supported some primitive life forms – a few small dirt-coloured fish with whiskery faces, and thin black eels, a specimen of which we once contrived to skin and boil in a tin can taken, like the water, from the river. We ate flakes of the off-white flesh. That was practising survival. What can one say of it now? That we survived is enough. Usually, on manoeuvres, we ran, crouched and jumped among the tumbled slabs and boulders of pit waste near the river's exit from the culvert at the foot of the lowering Squint tip, terrain as testing as any military range. Although it was unfenced, we had sense enough not to stray on to the colliery surface in the busy area between the engine house and the entrance to the drift, but we were often close. No one seemed concerned.

The mountain was better. George, lean and leggy, led us all over the mountain. My mother told me how she would follow our progress up the steep slope behind the house until we passed out of sight, wondering whether she would ever see me again, but she never asked what we'd been doing, out of her view for hour after hour. Wherever George led, Trevor, who was rounder and softer, more like his mother, was expected to follow, and when he wouldn't or couldn't, George bullied him with taunts and cuffs. Perhaps it was the treatment he had received at the hands of his older brother, Billy. He never raised finger or voice to me as I struggled to keep up.

One might have expected the episode with the petrol can to have taught him circumspection, but there was no evidence of it. He had a nerveless daring that sometimes terrified us. The apotheosis of his leadership was our longest expedition, which might possibly have been our last, for I can remember no other. It began with a trek to the trig point on the big tump at the top of the valley, not in itself unusual. There were four of us, including Dai Lester, gathered around the concrete plinth, taking turns to be hoisted on top and stand there surveying the moor spread about us, when someone noticed a black cloud approaching, not in the sky but about ten feet off the ground, a dense black cloud. As it neared we stared at it, trying to understand, until it was only a few yards away.

'Flying ants,' George yelled, and we ran like mad things in the opposite direction, pell-mell down the steep slope. By the time we reached the bottom the cloud had disappeared, but that was how we found ourselves on the path towards Penrhiwfer pond. We had visited the pond, a disused reservoir, before. It was a lovely sheet of calm water looking up at the sky from an asymmetrical saucer-shaped depression among rounded hills a hundred feet or so below the level of the moor. At one end was a little sluice where the dammed water escaped in a silver gush. We knew that if we followed the stream, as we had done on other occasions, it would lead us to Ghost Town – the ruins of Penrhiwfer Colliery.

The buildings of Ghost Town, of pale-red brick and roofed with slate, were so complete that from a little distance only the silence told it was not a working pit. But the windows had all been smashed, the engine house stripped of machinery, and the multitudinous metal parts that once littered the surface – drams, rods, girders, rail track, chains, wires – had all been removed. The nearest houses, a few straggling terraces, were some distance off and no sound came from them. We were alone there; our voices echoed in the emptiness. The two circular shafts were open to the sky. They had not been capped but were enclosed by brick walls about four feet high. The cement had begun to decay and bricks low down in one of the walls had loosened and fallen away leaving a hole at ground level through which a boy could easily thrust head and shoulders and peer into the depths. And this is what we did, lying full length and leaning through. Perhaps twenty feet down, light enough from a fine summer's day revealed stout steel beams at odd angles wedged against the sides of the shaft. They might have been parts of the dismantled winding gear that once towered above it, or scrap dumped from elsewhere on the site. Pit darkness soon enveloped the criss-crossing girders and beyond was a core of impenetrable black plunging hundreds of feet, which would rise up as daylight retreated.

Something seemed alive in the depths; we could hear it chuckle. George said if we dropped stones and counted how long they took to hit the bottom, we could work out how far they fell. We each dropped a stone, listened and heard a distant, faint splash. Ten ... fifteen – depending how quickly you counted – but it was a long way, a terrifyingly long way. As we pondered this, George did something very strange that I shall never forget. With a little effort he heaved himself up onto the two-bricks-width rim of the wall and laughed as we leant back on our heels and looked up at him standing against the sky and the old colliery buildings. We dared not speak, although we fervently wished he would come back to us. But he didn't; he walked around the crumbling top of the wall as though along a broad footpath and then stood and calmly looked about him, and perhaps saw the tears in our eyes, and with a show of reluctance, jumped down.

'Let's go to Bopa's,' he said. Whether a true aunt to George and Trevor, or merely an old, esteemed friend of the Vaughans, I cannot say, but I knew Bopa lived in Penygraig. 'She'll give us a drink,' added George and set off for the road that led from Penrhiwfer to the Rhondda townships.

It was the same road, the only road so far as we were aware, that the buses travelled to and from Gilfach. It led us through Williamstown and half a mile or so farther to Penygraig. Bopa's house was in a terrace close to the junction of our road with one that followed the river, the Rhondda Fawr, down to Porth. Anticipation of the drink we would have there had increased our thirst. George knocked at the door and we waited: no answer. He knocked again and shouted through the letterbox. Still no answer; Bopa wasn't in. Should we wait – but for how long? George said we could explore down by the river and, after a bit, return to the house to see if she'd come back.

We scrambled down an uneven slope to the river, as black as the Ogwr Fach, but much wider, and found there, just at the water's edge, a big cast-iron pipe running towards Porth. It must have been four feet or more in diameter and, although curved, its rust-pitted upper surface was broad enough to walk along, a far easier route than the riverbank, which had crumbled here and there. George set out along the pipe and we followed. The steep slope rising directly from the bank was crowned by a long row of houses and ashes and household rubbish had been poured down it for decades. That was not the source of the foul stink we became aware of as we walked; it came from pools of raw sewage that seemed to have been sweated from the base of the pipe. We were already sick of the adventure when someone noticed a gambo close to the foot of the tip. It was big and sturdily built – might seat three at a stretch – and would have been fast, but one of its four pram wheels was badly buckled, and that was clearly why it had been tumbled down the tip, unwanted. George wanted it, already seeing it repaired and speeding down High Street. We pulled and pushed the gambo up the steep tip, through a gap between terraces and on to the Porth road, where we stood, filthy and dishevelled. The sun was just beginning to sink behind the nearer houses by the time we had hauled the limping gambo to Penygraig. With our burden the route over the mountain was impossible; ahead lay the prospect of almost nine miles by road. Perhaps by that time I was showing signs of distress, if not actually weeping; or, perhaps George was seized with an uncharacteristic pang of human kindness, or yet again, he may have seen I would be an additional burden, slowing their progress with the gambo. Like a wounded soldier in an advance column, or a retreat, I would be left behind. He searched his pockets and produced two pennies, and Dai had another, together enough for the fare to Gilfach. I was left at the bus stop in Williamstown while they struggled onwards. I remember nothing of the rest of the day. I suppose I caught the bus and reached home as the sun stood above the western rim of the valley and our front windows reflecting its glow seemed lit brilliantly from within. My mother would have been relieved to see me; whether I was allowed to have tea before a bath is doubtful.

I heard the rest of the story from George and Trevor a day or so later. They had managed to drag the gambo as far as Penrhiwfer, where they were stopped by a policeman, who wanted to know what they were up to. He took names and addresses, confiscated the gambo and sent them on their way. It was already dark when, footsore, they reached home. All the effort had been for nothing, except to leave in our minds the memory of an adventure, still fresh in its essentials, after almost seventy years.

***

The bomb on the mountain was the last, indeed the only, direct assault on Gilfach, but sirens continued to sound air-raid warnings and all-clears. An air-raid shelter of brick and reinforced concrete was built on waste ground at the bottom of Glamorgan Terrace, thirty yards from our front gate, but never used. Its wooden doors remained locked, until at last, long after the war, it was demolished. In the early years we carried gas masks, lights were dimmed, the blackout was policed. My father had become a special constable in August 1938, as the discharge certificate dated 24 July 1942, which he had carefully preserved, later told me. He was Special Constable No. 421 B, an unpaid assistant to our small local police force. How often he went on duty, or whether he did so at all, I cannot say. The first I knew of his voluntary participation in the war effort was when, several years after the end of hostilities, a George VI medal with a smart red, black and white striped ribbon arrived through the post. It was awarded 'For faithful service in the Special Constabulary'. My father's smile was not so much of satisfaction at this tardy recognition, as puzzlement, the more so when he saw inscribed on the rim of the medal 'Sergeant T. S. Adams'. No one had told him he was a sergeant. Time enough had passed for us to receive this reminder of the war as a joke.

Inside our front railings, when I was young, was a privet hedge, trimmed tall at the gate pillar and gradually diminishing in height so that, like our railings, it presented a horizontal to passers-by. At the lower end a hurrying boy sent on an errand up the road ('You run and we'll count to see how quick you can be!') could step over hedge and fence on to the wall ledge and, with a little jump, to the pavement, saving a walk down the path and through the gate of fully twenty feet. It was usually to Joe Bacchetta's, to buy cigarettes. Eventually a brief rutted path crossed the strip of grass to the hedge at that end, the privet became thin and ragged, the wall sagged outwards and the mortar bedding the fence into the low pillar trickled purple dust. I don't remember when the hedge was hacked down and its roots dug up.

The front walls of the house were light brown from the cream and brown and ochre of the pebble-dashed rendering. The central portion projected under the inverted V of the roof and, on either side, set back, was a stubby wing. That to the right, viewed from the front gate, could be briefly lit by evening sun before it sank behind the mountain to the west, but otherwise lay in shadow. On the left a rather shabby porch had been added to shelter the heavy front door, half glazed with pink glass obscured by what appeared a myriad tiny craters or explosions. From the gate, looking up the curved path, visitors would not see the porch, but might be conscious of being overlooked by the large windows of two downstairs sitting rooms and the bedrooms above, each comprising four stoutly-framed, tall casements surmounted by lights of the same pink glass as the front door. The casements were opened only on the hottest days. When I think of them from within, it is with raindrops gathering and coursing down, and a sense of frustration, or sometimes etched with frost. Behind the front door lay a square hall, floored with glossy red tiles, where hung a gilt-framed painting of Highland cattle beside a loch. Above the hall was the smallest bedroom, my childhood bedroom. Abed there in the morning, I would sometimes hear the postman, or Reg Jefferies with the newspapers, climb the path towards the door and as the letterbox rattled the sound of claws skidding over the hall tiles and a loud thump as Dinah, our mad dog, hit the door and caught papers or letters in her slavering jaws.

In the centre of the broader portion of front lawn was a neglected circular flowerbed, so overgrown it might have been the remains of an Iron Age settlement viewed from the air. The path was of earth tamped hard, strewn with gravel, ochre, cream and brown, though patched here and there in the shade of the privet with velvet cushions of bright green moss. Perhaps while my grandfather lived the gravel was occasionally renewed. I saw it grow thin and the bare earth eroded dendritically. When my mother became wheelchair-bound, the path was concreted over to allow her to be wheeled in and out. But she rarely left the house when she had legs and afterwards sensitivity or pride would not permit her to pass beyond the door.

The house and its gardens, front and back, were separated from the neighbouring properties on either side by walls of local stone, rugged grey-green, pocked with lichen like splashes of molten brass and pewter, where snails' silver trails coalesced in niches. That to the left of the porch as you approached the house I remember almost hidden by a dense rose bush, a rambler with perfumed, bright pink flowers. Unfed and untended, it blossomed less and less abundantly, until eventually it too was hacked down and burned like any bramble.

Past the porch, the boundary wall was a high, dark cliff. Heavy footfalls on the narrow path paved with concrete flags that ran between it and the side of the house echoed strangely. Almost at the end of this canyon, a wooden gate with catch and bolt kept in the child, Barbara's handicapped boy, another victim of the war I think now, and Dinah, whose vicious disposition demanded caution on the part of any caller. At the gate strangers might think they had reached a dead end, for on the other side, before them, was the redbrick wall of a lean-to, slate-roofed lavatory backed against the rugged vertical, but to the right there, around the corner, was a back yard of purple paviours deeply incised with diamond channels for cane brush and sluicing water.

Low in the windowless back wall, a stubby lead pipe, shaped at the end like a kettle spout, brought waste water from the kitchen to a sink. The kitchen, as important to us as the omphalos of ash and flickering flame to our hutted ancestors, lay behind a stout wooden door that was opened by a simple latch. Two heavy bolts inside would have given security enough, but the door, its weathered green paint dull, was rarely bolted. A step or two across the yard from the doorway, to the left, was the lavatory; three or four steps to the right, the dark opening of the coalhouse. Just beyond the coalhouse was the big, iron-framed mangle with wheel and handle for turning. I remember sheets emerging stiffly from its heavy rollers. Between lavatory and coalhouse was a whitewashed wall of stone topped with a row of red bricks on end like well-spaced teeth. In the small square of garden behind the bricks each year a clump of Russell lupins thrust up dark blue and white spikes from a crowd of green hands with silver-haired spread fingers.

The doorless coalhouse, cut back into the garden, brick-built and flat roofed with corrugated sheets painted red, was big enough to hold a ton of coal and leave space where blocks of wood, the off-cuts of pit props, which my father brought up from the colliery, could be chopped for the fires. I see him now kneeling in that doorway, the small, keen axe smacking the stubby, resinous block and the pale sticks, some edged with bark, spilling cleanly on the paved floor. When he put the coal in, carrying it from the ton load dumped by the lorry outside our back gate along the garden path and down three steps into the yard, he would first build a wall of big lumps and pile bucketful after bucketful of graded smaller coals behind it so that the finer rubble was always on top at the back. When he had finished, in that almost pit-dark place, a new load presented a wall of coal like a fragment of a seam restored. Later, lazier, coal carriers raised a couple of nails securing a corrugated sheet and swung it back so that they could drop in lumps and empty buckets of small coal randomly through the roof. Out of the darkness seeped the throat-clogging exhalation of piled coal, like ancient rot. That I became accustomed to, but it was long before I lost my infant terror of the darkness and startled disgust at the black pats, elongated ovals of jet, the coal-coloured cockroaches, which scuttled invariably towards me.

The scruffy square of grass we called the back lawn was enclosed on three sides by the L shape of the house and the stone wall that separated us from the Lesters, our next door neighbours on that side, whose son and grandson, Dai, was my first friend. I cannot recall that dividing wall without the pair of wooden ladders, tall enough to reach the house roof, hung at an angle against it. Some time later, when my father had given up the shed on the old tip and the pits were closed, wedged into the corner between wall and house was a large crate on end, like a sentry box, where he kept a lifetime's accumulation of tools for all conceivable uses, an upright chest full of frustration after the accident that deprived him of the use of his right hand.

Six windows looked out upon that square of green from rendered walls, once smoothly white but increasingly over the years scabbed with neglect and clumsy repairs. The sash cord of the window that brought light into the back kitchen was broken, but it could be opened and propped ajar with a stick. On the broad outside sill of this window stood a sweet jar in which, each spring, I put some pond water and a blob of frogspawn, and once a solitary newt, until overnight rain unwontedly heavy even for Gilfach filled the jar to overflowing and the captive disappeared.

The bedroom sash window overlooking the garden was the largest in the house. When, later, I slept in that room I remember how the broad expanse of glass rattled ominously on windy nights, and how on one occasion, I was first stirred and then suddenly wide awake to the noise of frantically beating wings and a dark shape colliding with furniture and walls, fluttering against curtains pale with dawn and flickering about my head. A starling had fallen or flown down the chimney, from which, the day before, after an unexplained dry stick had appeared in the small fireplace, my father had pulled down and removed bucketsful of twigs, rags, clothes pegs, sheep's wool and moss. Below this bedroom window was a half-glazed door and a stone doorstep level with the grass. On fine days, the door would be open and in the doorway my mother would sit, knitting, crocheting, embroidering, studying racing form – or looking at the garden.

At the further end of the back lawn, a raised flowerbed marked the beginning of our garden, which sloped gently towards the house and was divided into almost equal parts by a roughly cobbled path. Halfway up the path was a tall iron pole, crusted red with rust, with a small pulley wheel at the top, over which the clothesline ran. A fork-ended wooden prop kept the line taut when washing billowed out on the smutty breeze. At the surface, the soil was black with decades of blown coal dust; beneath, it was heavy red clay. Seasonally, during my young childhood, loads of straw-strewn manure from the stables was forked in and the garden was cultivated. For a time old Sam Davies came to turn the soil and plant seeds. He was white-bearded and wore a bowler hat, and he toiled slowly in waistcoat and shirtsleeves, his broad-belted trousers tied at the ankles with string. When he paused to mop his brow and smoke a pipe, we would talk together. He showed me the ants' nest among the potato rows, how busy the tiny red creatures were, and how they worked together to overcome difficulties. If we were to separate one part of their community from the other by a channel filled with water, he told me, and if then we laid a spent match near this obstacle, the ants would push and drag the match until it bridged the stream and made them one again. That was when I was very young, before I started school, but I think I still believe it.

One side of the garden was largely given to cabbage, lettuce, leeks, radishes, the other to potatoes, onions, beetroot and a row of kidney beans aloft on rustic poles. It was just there, in the green shade of the twining bean shoots, that my mother and I secretly dug a hole with a trowel to hide the small, heavy biscuit tin with a pair of Scotty dogs on the hinged lid that she feared was full of bullets. I don't know how many years later I realised we had buried a box of lead shot, which my father was keeping – like so much else – against the possibility the lead would one day be useful. And, indeed, there was a time, during the war, when he melted lead from some other source in an old saucepan on the kitchen fire and, with a borrowed mould, turned out a battalion of running tin-hatted Tommies with bent rifles, which, even in those days of shortages, were heavy and unconvincing and soon discarded. Later, my mother did her gardening by proxy from her wheelchair. For her, a few rows of flowers were grown from seeds, usually sweet williams, but her favourite was the double white lilac at the top of the garden, against the back wall. She watched it carefully. Its first buds were a sign of spring advancing and she would not have to wait long to see the brilliant white cones of blossom shine out against the green of the mountain and tarry black of Mrs Driscoll's ramshackle chicken cots across the lane.

Halfway down the garden, close by the neighbours' wall, a clump of rhubarb unfurled each spring. My father upturned a bottomless bucket over it until stiff fibrous rods hoisted dark green leaves above the rusted rim. One of my clearest early memories is of sitting with Dai Lester on the doorstep of the house next door. We each hold, in one hand, a glossy crimson stick streaked with green and, in the other, sugar in the clipped corner of a dark blue Tate & Lyle paper bag.

We dip the rhubarb into the sugar, bite the tart, stringy stuff and feel the peculiar furring that such astringency brings to tongues and teeth.

The back garden gate was of heavy iron, spiked at the top and rusted like the clothesline pole, and outside, a massive iron slab, red and scabrous, bridged a shallow ditch to the lane. When at last and with great difficulty she had been persuaded to yield up the mauled newspaper and any letters she had caught earlier as they dropped through the letterbox, crazed Dinah sniffed about the garden on fine days. No one would have dared enter while she patrolled. Her jealous territorial guardianship extended beyond the wall, so that anyone who chanced to pass by outside, or even along the mountain path a hundred yards off, was howled at until they were out of sight. After Dinah's days, our garden, like those of our neighbours, was raided by the sheep that roamed freely everywhere in the valley. The gaps between the gate bars were too narrow for a grown sheep to squeeze through, but lambs could manage, and then the ewes would leap the stone wall. In a few hours, sheep could browse a garden almost to bare earth. My father strung wire along the top of the wall and wove a section of corrugated sheeting in and out of the gate bars until no gap remained. The gate, heavier still, opened and closed with prolonged terrible groaning like the entrance to a haunted castle. And still sometimes sheep got in. One spent an entire bitter, snowy winter sheltering in the patch where the lupins grew. And for a while her lamb would return there as to its home. By then the depredations of sheep meant nothing: the four ducklings that Joan, the older of my sisters, brought home in a shoebox from Cardiff market, given the freedom of the place, had nibbled with their exquisite bills until no green shoot remained.

Throughout the time I was growing up and for many more years, long after I had left home, apart from becoming shabbier, the exterior of the house changed hardly at all. Lacking the money to employ others to maintain the property, or two good hands to do it himself, at length, bitterly I am sure, my father ceased to care about appearances. He still raised ladders to the roof to repair guttering or replace slipped slates, clinging with his one good hand and forcing tools to a kind of grip between the useless fingers of the other, where they rubbed blisters, bloodily but painlessly, because the nerve-endings had been destroyed.

Indoors, furniture and the coverings of floors and walls changed, but not often. In my earliest recollection, the middle kitchen had a huge black range against the chimney wall with ovens and hobs arranged around an open fire basket, but I don't remember the fire lit, or cooking in that room. There, however, was the tall, glazed cupboard where crockery was kept, and the smaller cupboard beneath for pots and pans. There, too, was the door to the pantry, which had two shelves and at the further end, under the slope of the stairs, a thick white-tiled slab to keep food cool. All the business of food preparation, cooking and – apart from rare, special occasions – eating went on in the back kitchen. The fireplace there had a hob where the kettle sang and a spacious oven on top of which a bundle of chopped sticks dried ready to start the morrow's fire and heat again the boiler to provide hot water. There, too, was a large, brown Belfast sink with a scroll pattern incised on its lustrous side, where vegetables were prepared and dishes, and often clothes, were washed.

A stout sliding door between the middle kitchen and the hall, though rarely used, could separate this workaday, domestic part of the house from the two sitting rooms, both comfortably furnished, which were not kept for occasions but in daily use. I can see now that the back kitchen was meant to be the scullery, where a maid performed domestic chores, while the middle kitchen, with range and pantry, was the cook's domain – though not in our time, or, I think, my grandparents'. It was a house planned for a professional man and his family with servants who lived out, because there would have been no bedroom for them, but had the benefit of a lavatory in the yard outside the back door. Upstairs was a family bathroom and a separate lavatory. I was unaware that most of my childhood friends did not have a bathroom, or a lavatory indoors. The turned balusters and rail that led upstairs were of dark, varnished wood and at the top, on the landing, enclosed a space like a pulpit. From here my cousin Bloom stood from time to time preaching hilarious nonsense to my sisters sitting on the stairs when they were all young. And I, too, once sat on the stairs below the pulpit, in a mote-filled beam of sunlight streaming through the landing window, singing to myself:

> Who would true valour see,
> Let him come hither;
> One here will constant be,
> Come wind, come weather;
> There's no discouragement
> Shall make him once relent
> His first avowed intent
> To be a pilgrim.

– the lovely hymn by John Bunyan, which we often sang in school. My mother, overhearing this, decided I should join the church choir.

Both front bedrooms were large enough for a double bed, a wardrobe, a mirrored dressing table and a marble-topped washstand on which stood a big bowl and jug – and still felt spacious. The furniture in the larger room was oppressively dark and grand, the wardrobe huge, so that when you stood close and looked up it seemed about to topple upon you. The dressing table fascinated for two reasons. By looking at the large mirror before me, and adjusting the narrower mirrors on either side, I found I could view myself roundly, perhaps as others saw me. Far, far more interesting than that, while exploring the contents of the smaller, deep drawers in the upper part of the dressing table, I found a polished leather holster, and if I did not at once recognise what that was,

I knew as soon as I opened the brass catch and the heavy revolver slid out. I realised it was not meant for me to see and, with what feelings of guilt I cannot imagine, I put it back into the holster and the holster into the drawer. But my curiosity could not allow me to stop there. On other occasions I held the weapon in two hands and watched the cylinder turn one notch as I pulled the trigger. More alarming, now I look back, in a neighbouring drawer I discovered several stubby brass canisters – pristine, gleaming – that fitted my palm and, so smoothly, the chambers of the gun.

I made these discoveries before the summer of 1940, when the Home Guard was formed, for then my father gave the revolver to Christy Phillips, a collier who, as a very young man, had fought in the First World War and, on that account, had been appointed officer commanding the Gilfach Goch contingent. It was his badge of office. From time to time during the war years, when he was in uniform, I saw the holster on his belt. The last time was at the Victory Parade, when the Home Guard marched by the saluting base, a small platform overloaded with representatives of the military, the church and the local council, which had been set up in our front garden, beneath a V-sign in crazily flashing lights suspended from the front bedroom window. I had no opportunity to hold the revolver again, because it was surrendered to the police in the post-war weapons amnesty.

I was four or five when I found the gun, old enough to read and remember 'Webley Mark VI' inscribed on it. How we came to own it, I don't know. I think it might possibly have come with the long leather coat, helmet and goggles flyers wore during the First World War, which my father had bought (who knows where?) as protection from the weather when he was out on his motorbike. Why did we keep a fully functioning military revolver and ammunition? Again I can only guess. My grandfather's shop had been robbed, though that was an inside job. Then my father, whose motorbike and sidecar was one of the few vehicles in private hands, regularly travelled to

Bridgend, with the police sergeant as passenger, to collect the pay for the colliers in the Squint. It was a large sum in cash. Perhaps Sergeant Hobbs carried the gun on those occasions, just in case. I don't know either, whether my mother, who was terrified of guns and bullets, ever suspected I had found them in the dressing-table drawers and secretly played with them.

Like the bedroom above, the front room downstairs was square, high-ceilinged and spacious enough for heavy Victorian furniture. The mirrors of a tall, ornate mahogany sideboard reflected infinitely the room to whoever chose to look there or in another large mirror opposite, over the fireplace. Cupboards in the sideboard hid our stock of books – a two-volume biography of General William Booth, founder of the Salvation Army; an immense Family Bible, also in two volumes; six volumes of a work on electrical and mechanical engineering which my father was meant to study, though I never saw him turn a page, and, hidden at the back of the double-size middle cupboard, the photograph album Barbara's husband, Leighton, an able seaman, gave her for safe keeping when he returned to the ship for its final voyage. To the left of the sideboard, a well-polished oak table with bulbous legs, which could be extended to seat a dozen, had its place beneath the casement windows. My mother's piano stood against the opposite wall, and before the tiled fireplace was a discreetly patterned green moquette-covered Chesterfield suite. It was a wonderfully comfortable room – and big enough for parties, which occurred from time to time during the war years, when my mother's sisters and their husbands visited.

Much of family life went on in the back kitchen. A big fire glowed there from dawn or earlier and all through the day, its gaudiness reflected in polished brass. The high mantelpiece was edged with a brass strip and supported brass candlesticks alongside the clock and a mirror, which I waited many years to use. A brass stand where saucepans simmered stood before the fire, straddling a polished steel fender, on which my father sometimes sat to lace or unlace his pit boots. The kitchen was warm and redolent of cooking food, drying resinous kindling and laundered clothing. Beside the fireplace and facing the back door was an armchair, at first a fine high-backed wooden chair. To the left of the chair, between the oven and the wall was a shallow, curtained alcove, the cwtch, with a shelf where polishes and dusters and shoe brushes were kept. When Dinah was a pup, she slept in a cardboard box underneath the shelf and this was the place she always bustled to with whatever she had seized from the letterbox. Having grown immensely fat and bow-legged, she squeezed herself into the space and so filled it that she presented only a broad black back as she slobbered over letters or papers. Most attempts to retrieve them were met with threatening growls, and she resisted bribes. Hungry or bored, she would leave them of her own accord eventually, or when Barbara, exasperated, would shout threats and beat the armchair behind the dog's head. Then with a shuddering eruption, pushing the chair sideways, she would back out and do a little clumsy dance around the kitchen, laughing, with jaws agape and tongue lolling, as though it had all been a game. It was in the cwtch, too, that she became the surrogate mother of the ducklings Joan bought in Cardiff market, licking them sticky so that they soon became grey and ugly. We sank an old zinc bath in the garden and filled it with water where they paddled round and round, lost the layer of dust and fluff that covered them and emerged surprisingly yellow again. Once, in season, surreptitiously, she got out or, against her steadfast principles, let some local Lothario in. Weeks later her sagging belly told us she was in pup. We wondered whether motherhood would confer maturity, sense of proportion. We should have known. The young were sleek jet black like her, lovable as helpless young things are. She submitted to being sucked, but flung them off at the first faint sound of a footstep approaching our doors. One she trampled on and killed in her haste to reach the letterbox. The four survivors, doubtless traumatised, turned out the oddest mongrels – long-legged, floppy-eared, rough-coated. We gave them away. And reports came back: they were all mad like her. Their owners, less long-suffering than we were, had them put down. Dinah had been bought as a pup when Barbara's boy was born. They were meant to grow together and shared the floor when Leigh was crawling. He could tumble over her, as infants do, tug her tail, even pull at her long ears. She would not snap at him; and later if their paths crossed, not knowing any better, he would grasp her roughly, but she never once turned on him. She would shake herself free of his clinging fingers and amble away. That, at least, I give her credit for.

When I was young, my mother sat in that armchair by the fire. It seemed that whenever I came in from school or play, she would be there, thin and worn with pain, her poor legs blotched and wasted, looking up as I entered with eyes of such love. To her right, the warped deal table against the wall has always in my memory a cloth spread and food laid. Above it hung a dark monitory engraving, 'The Fruits of Idleness'. I have only to close my eyes to see again the wretched hovel it pictured, the distraught woman and sick child and, in the left foreground, the poacher husband with his gun and dog, and the dead rabbit hanging by its back legs. It represented the dread consequences of a life lived without a will to work and get on, qualities which Mam and Dats, my grandparents, had in abundance, and which had brought us the fine, comfortable house we lived in. Their son, my father, inherited the same work ethic along with the house. He could not stand idlers. The print might possibly have been from a painting by George Morland, who, unusually for an eighteenth-century artist, portrayed the rural poor. If it were after Morland, that would mean a great deal to me, but it disappeared long ago and there is now no way of knowing. Above the engraving an airing rack was suspended, usually decked with the day's washing. From time to time in the early years of the war, a quarter of bacon hung a few feet from it, on one of the two hooks in the ceiling. Who supplied it, I have no notion – someone my father knew, who occasionally killed a pig without informing the appropriate authorities and sold the meat on the black market. I believe there were elements of old friendship and quid pro quo in this arrangement, though my father had nothing to trade other than his skill with machines. The bacon was mostly fat with a gently curved sliver of pale pink lean running through it, but once thick cut with a carving knife, the salty reek of it cooking in a heavy pan over the open fire awoke a primeval appetite.

For a time, Aunty Olga and her son, my cousin, who was also John, lived with us. It was during the war. Uncle Gordon, my mother's youngest brother, then in his early thirties, was a captain in the army, the RASC I believe, and perhaps it seemed safer to bring his wife and child to Gilfach rather than leave them in a town, though which town I have no idea. John Love was a handsome child with fair curly hair – about six months older than me, but taller and as a town child a good deal more worldly wise. I think I resented his presence, and certainly we fell out from time to time. On our way home one evening, while we were climbing the familiar rough path from the Squint up to the railway crossing, bickering led to stone throwing. I was further up the path and the lump of coke I threw would have done no harm if he had not chosen that moment to stoop for another stone. It struck him just above the top lip. The blood terrified me. When I last saw John, many years ago, he had a moustache. I knew it hid a white Y-shaped scar. He also plays a part in one of my warmest memories of the back kitchen. We are up early. It is winter and still dark outside. My father has lit the fire, and he is there, not at work: it must be a Sunday. The fire is roaring in the chimney and its red glow is reflected in every polished surface and the black, blank window opposite the grate. My father puts the big frying pan with its layer of congealed bacon fat on the flames. He cuts two slices of bread from yesterday's stale loaf and dampens them slightly under the tap, patting the moisture in, and drops them in the bubbling fat. In a few minutes the bread is brown and crisp outside, soft within. He spreads the slices with jam for us. It is the very best fried bread, but John Love slips his crusts under the table where fat Dinah is waiting.

Eventually, after the war, the big fireplace was superseded by one somewhat smaller, and appurtenances of modern living moved in – a primitive washing machine with wringer attached next to the kitchen sink and, later still, an electric cooker, which allowed my mother to cook from her wheelchair. Change rippled out elsewhere. A refrigerator found a convenient place in the middle kitchen close to the pantry door. Later still it was joined by a splendid radiogram replacing the ancient wireless, which had long exasperated my father by losing its way among the wavelengths in a chaos of static crackle that could only be cured by a solid thump on the polished side. Finally television, installed in the front room, brought my mother there to watch the racing in the afternoon, and everyone for the evening's entertainment.

A conventional fireplace with marble pillars and mantelpiece replaced the great black range in the middle kitchen when I was very young, and it must have been the promise of greater convenience in lighting fires and raising ashes rather than a desire to improve appearance that brought to the back room the insipid mass-produced grate in pale brown and cream tiles. The original was particularly attractive, the fire basket set in an arch of red tiles, which also decked the kerb and gleaming hearth. Above the arch, an elaborate surround of dark polished wood formed three neatly panelled alcoves surmounted by the mantelpiece. And above the mantelpiece hung a giltwood framed circular mirror. I remember the creaking basket chair there, comfortably placed before the fire, the heavy bed settee covered in some dark grey tweedy fabric, and the oak dresser with open shelves above that was moved into the middle kitchen when the back room became a bedroom. At least the mirror held its familiar place while my parents lived, and the surprise of seeing it again recently, after a gap of thirty years or more, for a moment whipped my breath away. My niece had given it wall space and cared for it after the death of her mother, my sister Joan. So it is now with Kitty and Angus in Avoch, high on the east coast of Scotland, in a fine stone house overlooking the Moray Firth. The last piece of furniture from the old house is here with us – the ornate Victorian sideboard, with the double door that Barbara's son Leigh damaged, and the mirrors above, which, because we do not have a big mirror above the mantelpiece, no longer reflect infinitely the room and its occupants.

Three

WHEN I SET out to gather what information I could about my paternal grandmother's ancestors, I did not for a moment consider it might involve researching slavery in the West Indies. However, three of Mam's great-uncles, children of George Williams, Rector of Llantrithyd, and his wife, sailed to different parts of that region, presumably in search of fortune, and regardless of the hideous fact of slavery. In the previous decade their venture would not have been possible, but the end of the Napoleonic wars inaugurated a wave of migration as the West Indies ceased to be a fighting zone between the British and the French. Furthermore, post-war depression and continuing economic uncertainty at home were good enough reasons for those able to travel to seek a better life elsewhere. The colonies offered land and opportunity for any ambitious to get on, among whom were middle-class professionals and a scattering of the gentry with visions of estates more extensive and richly fertile than Britain could afford, incentives enough to put wind in the brothers' sails. And the timing was right – though not for George, the pioneer, whose death in Tobago in February 1815, was *before* the fall of Napoleon. True, the most eager colonists might have set sail during the fifteen months that separated the emperor's Elba exile in April 1814 and his return to face final defeat at Waterloo, 18 June 1815, but perhaps a more obvious reason for his presence on Tobago was that he was a soldier or a seaman. The Dutch and, with some ferocity, French, British and American forces had long disputed Tobago, a small, well-watered and beautiful tropical island with a hilly spine. It became British again in March 1793 when 2,000 men under General Cuyler took possession, and would have been garrisoned to fend attackers for twenty years after that. During the years of war, George's father was chaplain to the Glamorgan Militia and on friendly terms with the commandant, Richard Aubrey, whose family had military connections. It might have seemed that a career in soldiering offered opportunities beyond the ordinary to the second son of a rector as, often enough, it did to the second sons of gentry.

Plantations of sugar cane, cotton and indigo, tended by African slaves, had existed in Tobago since the seventeenth century, but economic development was interrupted from time to time by the depredations of those rival powers in the region. Under British control at the end of the eighteenth century, with trade re-established, windmills supplied power and sugar and cotton production in particular flourished. This was the settled island George would have experienced, albeit briefly. The likeliest cause of his death was dysentery or fever. The high mortality rate among slaves on the island had been debated in Parliament in 1797, opponents of slavery arguing that it was the inevitable result of a brutal regime, while its supporters claimed it was due to debilitating and often mortal illnesses, endemic in the tropics, which afflicted Europeans as much as slaves.

Demerara, part of a large administrative county in British Guiana, was situated near the mouth of one of three major rivers, which had together created an alluvial plain extending some thirty miles inland. Nineteenth-century maps show how this richly fertile region had been divided into parallel 'allotments' – strips of 500 or 1,000 acres – along the banks of the rivers and the coasts between their mouths to create some 350 plantations. Visitors in the 1830s would have observed many houses raised on piles close to the river, wind-powered or steam-driven sugar mills, coffee plantations with huge barns for the crop, brick-surfaced roads, hospitals, public buildings and barracks. We cannot tell when George's brother Philip – the younger by three years – arrived there, but he was well settled by the mid-1830s, for in 1836 he married Mary Seymour Thomas, then twenty-three, the daughter of 'James

Thomas, Gent.', clearly a possessor of wealth and influence, who probably owned the Thomas plantation (now part of the Tobago National Park) and whose London address was Upper Belgrave Place, SW1, where today foreign embassies cluster. The match suggests that Philip was a man of substance in the colony, though in what capacity we have no way of knowing. Owners usually had lawyers or plantation managers to represent them; perhaps he had advanced his career and standing by that route.

Jamaica, where Owen Glendour, the third and youngest of the brothers, sought his fortune, was by all accounts an island of great beauty in the nineteenth century, and no doubt still is. One hundred and fifty miles long and fifty-five broad, R. M. Martin's contemporaneous account describes it as a wonderfully varied landscape of 'high mountains ... vast savannahs or plains, hills and vales, rivers, bays and creeks', rich soil and abundant supplies of water. The climate was said to be 'not inimical to the human constitution ... evident from the long lives and good health which Europeans and negroes enjoy' – if they avoided the dangers of intemperance. By 1839 yellow fever had *almost* disappeared, a highly organised administrative structure was in place based on three counties, Middlesex, Surrey and Cornwall, each of which had a strong military presence, and there were substantial coastal towns benefiting from trade with Britain. Exports each year included 700,000 tons of sugar, 9,000 tons of excellent coffee and 3.5 million gallons of rum. This was the thriving tropical island that Owen, perhaps the cleverest of the brothers, found, but did not live long to enjoy. I have no doubt the sophisticated and wealthy white society there would have welcomed him for his skills as surgeon, and am left to ponder whether yellow fever carried him off at the age of thirty-six – or was it the rum?

The evident prosperity of these colonies, manifest in the great houses of the plantation owners, was founded upon a workforce of slaves, about 12,000 on Tobago in the early

1830s, 74,000 in Demerara, and 300,000 on Jamaica. In general they outnumbered the white populations by ten to one. Some of the data published in Martin's *Statistics of the Colonies of the British Empire* (1839) are staggering. In the eighteenth century it was calculated that 'Jamaica required an annual supply of 10,000 slaves to provide against the wear and tear of life'. One Jamaican owner supplied the information that on his estate of 2,200 acres he had 153 slaves. The number and persistence of slave revolts explain the continuing presence of military garrisons in all three colonies, long after victory at Waterloo and subsequent treaties had ended all outside threats. In Demerara, on 18 August 1823, a coordinated rising of some 13,000 slaves, from thirty-seven of the 350 plantations, led to the death of a few white managers and overseers. In an encounter with garrison troops a day later, 250 were killed, while one soldier was slightly wounded. Following a 'court martial' that began on 25 August and continued in various locations into 1824, more than 200 slaves were executed by hanging or shooting and their severed heads displayed on stakes. This was the barbaric end to an episode where for the first time slaves who were members of church congregations had played a prominent part. An Anglican priest, the Reverend John Smith, who had been consulted by insurgent leaders and had advised them to lay down their arms, was accused of inciting rebellion and sentenced to death. A successful appeal to the British government did not save him: he died of pneumonia in prison.

In Jamaica, nineteen slave insurrections occurred in the eighteenth century and five in the nineteenth, the last beginning on Christmas Day 1831, when an estimated 60,000, inspired by a Baptist preacher, Samuel Sharpe, himself a slave, went on strike. In the face of repressive action by white owners, the strike protest became violent. Plantations were burned and looted for several days until the military put down the rebellion. Fourteen white people were killed in the fighting and 300 slaves. Three hundred more slaves were hanged, including Samuel Sharpe.

That had been the pattern repeated for well over a hundred years: revolt answered by bloody repression and followed by trials and executions when a semblance of order was restored. In Britain reports of these terrible events influenced opinion among the public at large and in Parliament. It was an appallingly slow process, but they contributed to the ending of the slave trade in 1807 when it became illegal to trade in the traffic of slaves from Africa to British colonies, although slavery continued among the black populations transported earlier. The Demerara uprising in 1823 aided the argument for putting an end to it, and that in Jamaica in 1831–2 could only have hastened the passing of the act for the abolition of slavery in August 1833, which became effective on 1 August 1834. There followed a period of so-called 'apprenticeship', when slaves were paid for their work, before they were finally declared free on 1 August 1838. It seems now extraordinary, if not damnable, that compensation, amounting in Demerara, for example, to £4.3 million, was paid, not to the slaves, but to their erstwhile owners.

Four

ALONG WITH A third share in the house at 27 High Street (after our parents' days), I inherited two stories and an eighteenth-century Bible. For all I know, most families preserve stories of how they once held a higher station in life, handing them down from generation to generation on a constant slope of social decline. For what they are worth, these are ours.

The first is long, because I had at the outset some documentary evidence and became increasingly intrigued as I found out more. With all the fragments of history that came to light, in the end it remains an unsatisfactory tale, because vital pieces of the jigsaw that would allow me to feel confident of family links going back into the seventeenth century and beyond are missing. Nevertheless, I have learned a great deal, and often feel tantalisingly close to a complete solution. No wonder it continues to fascinate me.

The story says 'we' once owned Merthyr Mawr, near Bridgend in the Vale of Glamorgan, an ancient village and beautiful landscape of woods and sand dunes, but lost it through bad management or gambling debts or the chicanery of others. I have always understood the story is connected to a Bible passed down in the family of Margaret Williams, my father's mother, which originally belonged to the Reverend George Williams, Rector of Llantrithyd in the Vale of Glamorgan, and was given to me by my cousin Bloom.

When I received it, the Bible was uncased and deteriorating. I had it rebound and it stands now among other eighteenth-century books on our shelves. It was published in Bristol in 1778 as a Family Bible and the rector must have bought it for that purpose. In the years following his marriage in 1789 he carefully entered the births of his children on the blank pages that back a series of copperplate prints. The listing of offspring is incomplete, because it begins with the birth of Philip (who would die im Demerara), the fifth child, 'born at Lantrithyd on Wednesday, 16 December 1795 – at a quarter past 4 o'clock am'. The Reverend George was very precise. It does not include Bloom, first of the nine children born to Sarah, the rector's wife, who was baptised on 22 September 1790.

Bloom, that unusual name, here given to my grandmother's grandfather, whom she knew in his old age, was preserved through three generations in our family as though it bore a special significance. It was the forename of Mam and Dats' first son, my Uncle Bloom, and of the first son of their daughter, whom I knew as Aunty Julia, my cousin Bloom. When I was an infant, he would catechise me in the following terms:

'What are those in the bowl on the table?'

'Strawberries.'

'No, they're not. They're bloody strawberries. What are they?'

'Bloody strawberries.' And so on.

He it was, anyway, who gave the Bible to me. There the name has stopped, for which our sons are grateful. I have long wondered where this oddity came from, but attempts to trace its origins have been unsuccessful. Another Bloom Williams, a contemporary of the rector, was well known in Cardiff as an apothecary and surgeon, and later as alderman and man of affairs, but I have not been able to prove a family connection between them, although they certainly knew one another as fellow magistrates of the county of Glamorgan. Perhaps there is a relationship further back, a common ancestor, or (far less likely it seems to me) it could be that the Reverend George had reason to hold Bloom, the apothecary, in high regard and could think of no better way to express gratitude and admiration than naming his firstborn after him.

I was told, and believe, there was another Bible, smaller and stouter than the one I have. It would have been

About 1900, Mam and Dats, Sam and Margaret Adams, and their children – Julia, Bloom and the youngest, Tom, who would be my father.

About 1922: four generations, Mama, our mother, with her mother, Mary Jane Love, and her mother's mother, Catherine Stokes (née Lewis), and her daughter, Joan.

Mama and Dada, Edith Love and Tom Adams, about 1919, before they married.

About 1913, our house in High Street, set back a little from the un-macadamised road. At the railings in the front are Rev. George Llewellyn, 'the blind vicar', his wife and daughter. The house was bought in 1916 by my grandfather, Sam Adams.

The last men in our close family to be given the name Bloom: my uncle, Bloom Adams, and my cousin, Aunty Julia's son, Bloom Trethowan, who gave me the Family Bible of our great-great-great-grandfather, Rev. George Williams, the rector of Llantrithyd.

My sisters – with Mam, about 1927, Joan on the left, Barbara on the right, and on holiday in Tunisia, probably in the 1970s, Barbara this time on the left.

Barbara about 1940, and her husband-to-be, Leighton Francis, able seaman, gunner.

Joan and Tommy, at the bar in the Griffin Inn, known to all as 'The Bog'.

With our boys, Nick and Jonathan, my mother in her favourite spot, the doorway of the back room, and another fat dog, Sally.

My father with Rhona and her foal. It is late in the 1940s; he is not using his right hand.

Late 1960s, in our back garden: Dada on the 1919 AJS, which he restored with one hand.

A classic view of a mining valley: Gilfach Goch about 1900. The long terrace overlooking the pit is called 'Fairview'.

GGH.33F   THE COLLIERY, GILFACH GOCH

Another very early view of Gilfach, from the north end, with pits developed to the west of the Ogwr Fach and developing to the east, and the straggle of terraces that would be consolidated into High Street running down the eastern flank.

Courtesy of Reflective Images

Foot Bridge, Gilfach Goch.

1920-30

Looking north, the White Bridge – a concrete pedestrian way from High Street to Evanstown, if you didn't mind skirting the colliery on one side and the foot of a colossal tip on the other. A path over the mountain to Clydach Vale and the Rhondda is clearly visible.

Pit engine houses kept the wheels on the colliery turning and gave energy to spare.

Off the road: a Rhondda bus, Gilfach's first motorised public transport, powered by electricity.

GGH 32F CINEMA AND BRIDGE, GILFACH GOCH

The way to school: past the Workmen's Hall, over the bridge, up Coronation Road, to the cluster of buildings against the mountain on the left.

Viewed from the north side and the south, the embankment made of a combustible mixture of colliery waste that carried the road from High Street to Evanstown, a culvert at its foot to channel the Ogwr Fach. By the 1940s it appeared volcanic and on wet days emitted stinking vapour clouds.

Another view just after collieries and railways disappeared

General View Gilfach Goch.900

Views towards the north, the middle ground occupied by a huge tip that buried a school and several houses – while the pits were still working, and after they were closed and dismantled.

The top of the valley, where mining was concentrated, cleared of collieries and tips, made green again.

published earlier in the eighteenth century, or perhaps it was older even than that, and originally belonged to the father of the Rector of Llantrithyd, namely, the Reverend George Williams, Vicar of Penlline. The common practice in earlier centuries of giving parental forenames to the children can be confusing, as it is here. However, the elder George, whose wife's name was Esther, would have inscribed the births of their eight children in that older Bible and (who knows?) given some indication of his own origins, so solving many of my problems, before it was inherited by his son. But, alas, it has disappeared. In the dispersal of effects following Mam's death, I believe both Bibles went to her eldest child, Julia (another recurring family name, as will be explained) and she in turn gave them to her eldest, Bloom, who presented one of them to me. I can only assume the missing Bible, perhaps even more dog-eared and shabby than the one I rescued, was simply thrown out as beyond repair and of no interest. Its loss is deeply frustrating, although, so far as the eight children of the Reverend George and Esther are concerned, it has not proved irreplaceable, for they were baptised at Ystradowen in the Vale of Glamorgan, and are listed in the parish register.

George, their firstborn, was baptised on 7 July 1763. I came across him next in a document dated 31 January 1786, lodged at the National Library of Wales, in which his father wrote as follows to 'Richard Lord Bishop of Landaff':

'I do hereby nominate & appoint Geo: Williams to perform the office of Curate in my Church of Penlline … and do promise to allow him the yearly sum of twenty pounds for his maintenance'.

His son was only twenty-two at the time, below the canonical age for ordination, but there could be exceptions to canon law and presumably one was made here. The most likely extenuating circumstance was the ill-health of the elder George, who died in August the same year. There is no evidence of the new curate's education. Perhaps the best one could hope for him is that he attended Cowbridge School. It was not uncommon at the time for clergymen to lack graduate status. The younger George succeeded his father as curate at Ystradowen also, and by 4 May 1788 he was officiating at Llantrithyd, for on that day he baptised one of the children of John Perkins of Pentra Farm there. Perkins was a gentleman farmer who became a close friend and, as we shall see, is an important contributor to this story because, from 1788 to 1801, he kept a diary.

The elder George Williams was interred within the church at Llansannor, as the following note reveals:

> Rev. George Williams, Vicar of Penlline, who lived at Upper Maendy in the parish of Ystradowen in the county of Glamorgan and diocese of Llandaff. Departed this life 5th August 1786 at 4 o'clock p.m. and was interred on the 7th within the chancel of Llansannor (the south side of it) by the Revd. David Griffiths, curate of Llanilid in the same county and diocese. Written by George Williams, son of the deceased.

When Perkins first writes about his new friend, it is as 'Geo: Williams of Mayndy', which suggests that young George had lived with his father at Upper Maendy, a farm not far from Ystradowen and only a couple of miles north-west of Llantrithyd, and that he continued to live there after his father's death. Subsequently it becomes clear that he knew a good deal about farming, and probably farmed his father's land both before and after becoming a curate.

We gather from Perkins' diary that George Williams was an amiable companion, with whom he shared many pleasant social occasions. That he made a favourable impression on people of wealth and standing is borne out by another document, from the Llandaff Cathedral archives, dated 19 August 1789, only three years after he had become a curate. In it, 'George Williams, Clerk, of Ystradowen' and his supporter 'Ambrose Portrey of Llanmaes, Gentleman', bound themselves in the sum of £200 to fulfil all conditions necessary to the marriage of George to Sarah Jones of Ystradowen, and a licence was issued accordingly.

The curate's connection with Ambrose Portrey is easily explained. The latter was of an old Llanmaes family, and Margaret Aubrey, who lived at Great House, Llanmaes, was a neighbour. A large part of the 7,000-acre Aubrey estate in the Vale of Glamorgan was leased to her, while Sir John Aubrey, the sixth baronet of Llantrithyd, lived on estates in Buckinghamshire that had come to the family by marriage. In the previous century, the same Aubrey family, who were his cousins, gave succour to John Aubrey, author of the *Brief Lives* – and in the same place, Llantrithyd, where (referring to himself in the third person) he recalled, 'He began to enter into pocket memorandum bookes philosophicall and antiquarian remarques, Anno Domini 1654'. Margaret Aubrey was unmarried, the matriarch of her clan, deferred to by all. Whether he had previously met George Williams or not, Portrey would have been glad to accede to her wishes. And Margaret knew Sarah Jones, the bride-to-be.

The marriage register of the parish church of Ystradowen tells us the wedding took place on 3 September 1789. Among the seven witnesses to the ceremony was Julia Frances Aubrey, the eight-year-old daughter of Richard Aubrey Esq., and his late wife Frances. Hers is the clearest signature. Ambrose Portrey and Richard Williams, George's younger brother, also a curate, are other identifiable signatories. *The Gentleman's Magazine* for September 1789 noted the event among its 'Marriages of considerable Persons' thus: 'At Ystrad-Owen, co. Glamorgan, the Rev. Geo: Williams, of Maindy, to Miss Sally Jones, of Ash Hall.'

Why did this marriage have a grand parade of seven witnesses? And why did the marriage of a humble curate, on the bottom rung of the ecclesiastical ladder, attract notice in *The Gentleman's Magazine*? George's bride, who was at least three years older (she died in 1853, aged 94), lived at Ash Hall which still stands a little distance from the hamlet of

Ystradowen, flanked by trees on a low hill. It is a large, elegant dwelling with symmetrically-arranged, tall sash windows and a long veranda shading the ground floor to the south-west. It breathes wealth and rank, and at that time was the family home of Richard Aubrey and his two children. Richard, youngest son of Sir Thomas Aubrey, the fifth baronet of Llantrithyd, had married Frances Digby, who died, aged thirty-one, in December 1782, within a week or so of giving birth to a son, Thomas. The infant and his two-year-old sister, Julia Frances, were the only surviving children of the marriage. The loss of his young wife must have been a terrible blow to Richard Aubrey. He did not remarry, but clearly a surrogate mother was needed for the children, to whom their upbringing and early education could be entrusted. It seems highly likely the choice fell upon Sarah Jones, whom the Aubrey family came to know as 'Sally'.

Sarah had cared for Thomas (who would become the seventh and last baronet of Llantrithyd) and Julia Frances for four years or more when she met the young curate at Ystradowen church, and in another two years friendship and mutual regard had become affection and attachment. There is no reason to believe the couple were other than happily matched, but a good deal more was at stake. Sarah's connection with the Aubreys meant that George was brought to the fringes of their circle. And then – on or about 28 March 1790 – at the age of thirty-nine, Nehemiah Hopkins, the incumbent Rector of Llantrithyd, died. This gave the Aubreys a timely opportunity to show their gratitude to a capable nursemaid, governess – and perhaps more – by ensuring she and her husband had a home, a livelihood, and a position in the community. It was a remarkable stroke of fortune for my great-great-great-grandfather, a relatively inexperienced curate, that he should be preferred as rector of a living worth some £120 per annum.

The parish of Llantrithyd extends over 1,400 acres, but there is no village, no cluster of dwellings with the usual inn and a few shops. The small population, probably 200 or so in the late eighteenth century, lived in scattered farms and cottages. Almost all the land was owned by the Aubreys, whose family seat, Llantrithyd Place, a splendid Tudor mansion said to date from 1546, stood in a small valley next to the church. The demesne included an array of stone outbuildings set in a garden with terraces, ponds and walks, and a walled deer park. Now, entrance to the remains of the house – fragments of blackened walls standing like a reef of rocks and stacks exposed by a receding green tide – is by a farm gate and through mud churned shin deep by cattle. It was abandoned in the 1820s. The roof fell in about 1832 and the fallen stone and timber were pillaged for the building projects of others. But it was still magnificent when the new rector passed by daily, and his church stands nearby, a small building of grey local stone dating from the late medieval period. It preserves within some exceptionally fine monuments to sixteenth-century landowners, the Bassetts and the Mansels, a number of memorial tablets for members of the Aubrey family, and one for George Williams and Sarah placed there by their youngest son, Thomas. The rectory appears as old as the church, but the original building burned down in the mid-nineteenth century. It was rebuilt much as before and, even today, appears rather grand.

John Perkins brought his growing family to Pentra Farm, Llantrithyd, in 1788–89, at much the same time as George Williams entered the rectory. Perkins was a member of the minor gentry, who had augmented inherited property by marrying a wealthy widow. I have reason to be grateful to him because I have been able to learn a little of the daily life of my three-times great-grandfather thanks to brief daily notes he made in his diary. They are rapid jottings with many abbreviations, eccentric use of capitals (as was common at the time) and a few consistent spelling errors. Every day he began with a note of the weather and, in addition to farming activities, he also recorded meetings with people of some significance, among whom he counted 'Geo: Williams'.

Perkins' friendship with the rector began almost at once and was lasting. By my count, George Williams is mentioned 316 times in the diary between 1788 and 1801. In 1793–94 they met on no fewer than 158 occasions and, though reported contact was less frequent after that, the warmth of the relationship continued. On 9 August 1799, for example, Perkins noted:

'Geo. Williams Dined with me on a neck of Venison [almost certainly a gift from the Aubreys' deer park] … in Eveng I drank tea with Geo: Williams he went with me to Leechcastle'.

Visits were exchanged frequently, involving not only the men but the wives and, to some extent, their children also. On 23 September 1792 Perkins took the trouble to record 'little Bloom Williams came up in Eveng with the maid', the first of twenty-two references to Bloom, in all but three by name. Bloom seems to have been the sort of child, perhaps old for his years, worth remarking. On 28 December 1793, when he was only three, Perkins wrote:

'in Morng Williams call'd … Williams's little boy & self went out a coursing cd not run a hare'.

References throughout the diary reveal how fond Perkins was of children. So, no doubt, were George and Sarah. It was just as well: the pattern of a birth each year, or very nearly so, continued until 1801, although three girls and a boy died in infancy. John and Bessy Perkins lost children too, and the grief of infant mortality brought the families closer together. On 31 July 1792 the diary tells us 'Mr Williams's child out of inoculation, died'. This was the first of two boys named George, probably born in 1791. On 12 March 1789, Bevan, the local doctor, had inoculated the Perkins children with smallpox pus, as was then the practice if parents were prepared to take the risk. They became very ill but, carefully tended by Bevan, they survived and were thereafter immune to the disease. The rector and his wife were less fortunate.

With the rectory came the glebeland, an unusually large area of about sixty-eight acres. Perkins' diary reveals that the rector farmed some of this land and leased other parts, and that they discussed crops and livestock and helped one another. Perkins also kept a notebook into which, among other things, he copied the official 'Valuation of Llantrithyd Parish' for 1805. Among the larger individual valuations we find 'Geo. Williams Clk Glebe & Tythes £126 0s 0d', but roughly, at the foot of the same page, Perkins made what appears to be a more complete valuation of the rectory and glebe:

Tythe & Glebe lets	260
House & 2 fields in Hand	21
	281

If this is accurate, the Rector was comfortably off; the valuation of Perkins's own farm and land holdings was set at £267.

Perkins was no doubt pleased to consider himself on familiar terms with close relatives of Sir John Aubrey, and indeed with the baronet himself, who, on 11 June 1798 gave him a barrel of beer and ten dozen bottles! Through Perkins' diary we know George Williams, too, was a member of the group. References to companionable outings, particularly hunting game, dining at Ash Hall, and other meetings and visits occur quite frequently:

3 September 1791 – 'went with Aubrey & Geo Williams a Shooting … they dined hear and went away tween 7 and 8 o'clock';

2 September 1794 – 'Col. Aubrey & Williams din'd hear & went away abt 9 o'clock';

14 September 1800 – 'went with Geo Williams in Eveng to Ash Hall'.

Among the friends were members of the Glamorgan Militia, of which Richard Aubrey was made commandant on 21 April 1794. George Williams probably became chaplain to the Militia at the same time. In this role he certainly accompanied the regiment on a tour of duty outside the county, as the following baptismal entry in the Llantrithyd register reveals:

'James Horatio son of William Vaughan Serjeant in the Royal Glamorgan Militia by Ann his wife was baptised at Bristol in the Messhouse on the 6th day of September 1806 by me George Williams Rector of this parish & Chaplain to the above Corps.'

If the chaplain was generally expected to ride with the regiment, he may well have accompanied it on tours of duty in the south and south-west of England, and in Ireland, at a time of threats from Revolutionary France and the Napoleonic Wars. It is not without significance that Sergeant William Vaughan's son was named 'Horatio'. Lengthy absences from Llantrithyd would explain why he and Perkins met less frequently after 1794. While he was absent, George's brother Richard, who was ordained deacon and immediately afterwards appointed curate of Llantrithyd in June 1793, performed the Rector's duties.

Among other diary entries to catch the eye are possible references to Sarah's family:

31 January 1793 – 'In Eveng Bessy, Maria & self drank Tea at Mr Williams's young Jones of Langan call'd there';

25 August 1793 – 'A fine day children all went to Church in Eveng. Mrs Williams, her brother & the children call'd in their way walking'.

Was there a Jones family of Llangan? And was Sarah a daughter? What, in sum, do we know of Sarah? Of her parents and background, nothing, but for many years I have believed that, if there is a smidgen of truth in the family legend that we once owned Merthyr Mawr, then the connection is through her. No member of her family can be clearly identified among witnesses at her wedding, which implies, if there were living relatives, they lived some distance away.

The presence of the eight- or nine-year-old Julia Frances

Aubrey on that occasion reinforces the impression of a special relationship with her. It is certain Richard Aubrey's daughter was affectionately remembered by the Reverend George and his wife, who named not one but three of their daughters after her – two baptised Julia Frances, the first having died young, and another some years later named Frances (her older surviving sister presumably being known as Julia). That name, Julia, like Bloom, echoes down the generations in our family. It was given to one of Bloom Williams's daughters, a great-aunt I never met, and, as already mentioned, by Mam and Dats to their firstborn.

The birth of George and Sarah's son Bloom is a puzzle. Why, when the marital home was in Llantrithyd, was Sarah's confinement in the parish of Coychurch? Surely she had a reason for leaving what must have been the relative comfort of the rectory, and the proximity of influential friends at Ash Hall. Could she, perhaps, have gone to her own people, anticipating from them the help a new mother might need? Coychurch is about twelve miles west of Llantrithyd (not far, though given the usual state of rural roads in those days, hardly convenient), but much closer to Llangan, and to Merthyr Mawr. And is it merely a coincidence that in March 1819, Bloom Williams, having inherited the Family Bible from his father, entered in it the birth of a daughter 'at Penalan in the Parish of Coychurch', naming her 'Frances Sarah'?

Here we need to consider the convoluted story of the Bowens and the Joneses who were owners of Merthyr Mawr towards the end of the eighteenth century. Hugh Bowen of Oystermouth married into the Stradling family of St Donats, which did not quite extend back to the Norman Conquest but was anciently wealthy. When Sir Thomas Stradling, last of the line, died in a duel at Montpellier, France, in September 1738, control of the estates passed to a cousin, Bussy Mansell. His death in 1750 precipitated an avalanche of lawsuits from rival claimants. Litigation continued for seventeen years and was only concluded by an Act of Parliament that sanctioned distribution of the estates by the drawing of lots. In this way Hugh Bowen inherited Monknash and Merthyr Mawr, the latter alone being valued at £5,000. His marriage being childless, Bowen bequeathed these properties to an illegitimate son, Charles, and he (in a will proved 13 April 1787) left them in trust. Three trustees were appointed and charged with the task of selling the whole of the estate, which was heavily mortgaged. After settling Charles's affairs by the payment of debts and a few smaller legacies, they were to invest the proceeds securely so that the interest thereof should support Bowen's wife, Catherine, while she lived. On Catherine's decease, whatever remained was to be given in equal shares to Thomas, Stephen and Ann Jones, Charles's half-brothers and sister.

Thomas appears to have been on good terms with Catherine, which is more than can be said for Stephen. His bitter opposition to her, which may have been caused, or at least exacerbated, by her remarriage in May 1796 to John Richardson of Merthyr Mawr, is revealed in an entry in the diary of John Bird, a Cardiff notable, concerning the death of Catherine in October 1798:

'Mr Stephen Jones refused to let her be interred in the family vault at Merthyr Mawr. He has taken Possession for himself and Sister of the Merthyr Mawr Estate.'

Thomas, the eldest of the siblings, having died, it was principally with Stephen Jones that protracted negotiations for the sale of Merthyr Mawr were conducted. So complicated were they that thirteen years elapsed before the decision was made to proceed and, in 1800, sale catalogues detailing the estate were printed. At that point, Stephen and Ann demanded a price far exceeding the valuation of the property. Further delays followed and there was a great deal of legal wrangling, the effects of which can be seen in a mass of documents now lodged in the Glamorgan Archives. Finally, in 1804, an agreement was reached by which one of the trustees of Charles

Bowen's will, Sir John Nicholl (a lawyer of considerable distinction, knighted in 1798), acquired Merthyr Mawr, an estate of more than 800 acres, for £18,000.

What relationship (if any) existed between the siblings Thomas, Stephen and Ann Jones and Sarah Jones there seems now no way of knowing. No proof exists of the story preserved in our family, but that does not mean it was a fiction. There must be a link, why else bother to preserve it?

The gossipy journal of David Jones of Wallington and Llanblethian (who was not a relative), affords a glimpse of the interior of the rectory at Llantrithyd when it was George and Sarah's home and the style in which they lived. He describes how, at an auction in Bridgend in 1885 or thereabouts:

'numerous fine pictures which had belonged to the Rev. Geo: Williams, in particular some fine George Morlands ... also paintings by other distinguished painters were sold for a few shillings each'.

Today, paintings of rural scenes by Morland can change hands at tens of thousands of pounds, and David Jones considered them worthy of special remark in the nineteenth century. George and Sarah evidently took pride in appearances and pleasure in art and were prepared to spend to indulge their interests. What then occurred on the death of the rector must have shocked the neighbourhood.

The Reverend George Williams, Rector of Llantrithyd, died on 21 December 1815, aged 52. This seems a sadly early death, but John Perkins was only 56 when he died on 10 June 1816. Perkins left a will sharing his substantial property among his children. His friend the rector, on the other hand, seems to have been unprepared to meet his Maker. That there was no will suggests that (whatever the cause) he died suddenly. He did, however, leave debts. A copy of a 'Principal Creditor Citation' dated 14 March 1816, obtained from the National Library, names Richard Lewis 'the principal creditor of the Reverend George Williams, late Rector of the parish of Lantrythid'. This notice, which was to be affixed to the church door at Llantrithyd 'during the time of divine service', further says:

'Sarah Williams and all and every the children of the said George Williams in special and all others in general having or pretending to have any right title or interest in the Goods Chattels and Credits of the said deceased [should appear before the Consistory of Llandaff Cathedral and, if they cannot show sufficient cause to the contrary] we ... will proceed to the granting and committing Letters of Administration of all and singular the Goods Chattels and Credits of the said deceased simply as dying intestate to the said Richard Lewis.'

We know little of this Richard Lewis beyond his claim on the rector's estate, but the public exhibition of indebtedness may well account for the poor reputation imputed to the Reverend George Williams in a manuscript history of Llantrithyd written several decades after these events by 'Ioan Trithyd'. Frequent absences due to service with the Militia would not have endeared him to parishioners either. I have learned recently the precise nature and amount of the debt in another document obtained from the National Library. It is an affidavit sworn on 14 March 1816 by 'Richard Lewis of the parish of Lantrithid in the County of Glamorgan, Yeoman' in which he deposes that he was owed 'the sum of ninety-six pounds of lawful money of Great Britain ... for wages as a servant in Husbandry'. Lewis signed his deposition with a cross; he was illiterate. The rector employed him to farm the glebe, or possibly Lewis contracted the work to others. Why he wasn't paid is a matter for conjecture, although, if George Williams died suddenly, as his intestacy strongly suggests, that would be the most obvious reason. The same Richard Lewis is probably the father of three illegitimate children whose births are entered in the parish register: Richard in September 1803, Ann in January 1804, and Aesop Charidemus in January 1806, all three by the same spinster, Ann John. The name of the youngest child suggests Lewis possessed imagination and ambition beyond the reach of the usual illiterate small farmer. The £96 he said were due in wages appears a similar imaginative leap, representing five or more years of toil on the land. There is no record of a consistory court hearing of his claim, which suggests a settlement was reached. In any event, widow Sarah would surely have been able to find the whole sum Lewis claimed, if it finally came to that.

Sarah and the children who were probably still at home – Julia Frances, Thomas, Owen Glendour and Julia, whose ages ranged from eighteen to fourteen – would have been obliged to leave the rectory as soon as the new incumbent was appointed. Of the other children, Bloom was probably farming his father's glebe and, if history could repeat itself, awaiting appointment as curate, though that possibility vanished with his father's death. He continued to be involved in farming and within a year was married and living at Pickett, near Llandow. At least two of the younger children accompanied their mother, in due time, to London, for twenty-five years later, in 1841, the widowed Sarah, Thomas and Thomas's daughter, Julia, were living at Albany Road, St Giles Camberwell, which curves north-east to a junction with the Old Kent Road. Not long before it had been a parish of market gardens, meadows and scattered villas, but the population was growing apace. The Williamses' neighbours included dressmakers, a stonemason and schoolteachers. I now know that, when he was sixteen, shortly after his father's death, Owen Glendour, was apprenticed for five years to an apothecary, Benjamin Gustavus Burroughs, in Clifton, Bristol. During his apprenticeship, he attended courses on anatomy and physiology, the theory and practice of medicine, chemistry and 'materia medica', and worked for six months at a hospital general dispensary. He brought this record and Burroughs's testimonial to his moral character with him to London where he was examined and, on 17 May 1821 at the age of twenty-one, received his licence to practise medicine (LSA) from the Worshipful Society of Apothecaries.

Perhaps on leaving Llantrithyd the family had first moved

to Bristol and it was only after Owen Glendour had completed his apprenticeship that they found a new home in London. In any event, the newly qualified surgeon did not long reside under his mother's roof. In 1823 he married Sarah Hughes, and the following year we find him in the process of dissolving a partnership with William Ankers as 'Surgeons, Apothecaries and Accoucheurs' at an address in the street known as Great St Thomas Apostle and setting up in medical practice on his own account, first nearby at Cloak Lane and then in Doughty Street. Cloak Lane and, especially, Doughty Street are significant addresses. Property in the latter sells at £4million and more today. When Charles Dickens brought his family to number 41 (now the Dickens Museum) in the 1830s, the street was gated with uniformed porters stationed at either end. We cannot tell whether Owen Glendour's partnership with Ankers broke over disagreements between them, or whether it occurred simply because Ankers was leaving London (he settled thereafter in Cheshire). Perhaps Owen Glendour glimpsed a promise of greater success working on his own, as the move up-market to Doughty Street might suggest.

It was only recently I found that he, who had seemed destined to become a prosperous member of London's professional middle classes, died in the West Indies. For this extraordinary turn of events a death notice in the *Cambrian*, 3 December 1836, tells all we are ever likely to know: 'Aged 36, in Jamaica, Owen G. Williams, Surgeon, son of Rev. G. Williams, Lantrithyd.'

To discover that one great-great-great-uncle died on a spot of land at the far south of the island chain of the West Indies was a surprise. That two equally unfortunate brothers followed him to the same distant part of the world just north of the Equator was singular indeed. And the sense of strangeness in this tale was accompanied by an uncomfortable realisation that they were certainly observers of the final decades of slavery and in all probability active participants, even if not for long and at the price of an early death.

My only sea voyages have been on cross-Channel ferries, probably no more than a dozen times, the longest Southampton to St Malo. On a few occasions the wind has been strong, the sea rough. I have never been seasick, but I dislike the experience intensely: the crowds of people, the constant thud-thud of the ship's engines, the perceptible tension of those for whom being on the sea is a nightmare. Would I have been more content to travel on a small wooden ship under sail? Just possibly; at this distance it has a romantic appeal. But on such a long voyage? George, Philip and Owen Glendour would have sailed west across the Atlantic, between 4,500 and 5,500 miles and, depending on wind and weather, it would have taken them about five weeks to reach journey's end – for all of them a final destination.

I am left with the odd fact that three of the five sons of a rector from the Vale of Glamorgan, while still quite young, died in the Caribbean region. Perhaps George, before he succumbed to whatever bore him off, sent home encouraging letters about prospects there and, in his turn, Philip did the same. It may be that Owen heard there were rich pickings to be had for a London surgeon among wealthy colonists in Jamaica. It is also just possible that all three were in flight from circumstances in Wales or London over which they had lost control. Whatever drove them all that way, into involvement in the history of the slave trade, and to early deaths, it is just a little reassuring that the stark notices of their passing suggest a sense of family and pride in their father remained strong in the survivors: death notices declare they were, all three, the sons of the Reverend George Williams and Sarah his wife, of Llantrithyd in the Vale of Glamorgan.

***

Sarah was described as 'independent' in 1841 and the 1851 Census tells us both she and her daughter, Julia Frances, had annuities, almost certainly from proceeds of the estate of the Reverend George Williams, after settlement of the debt to Richard Lewis. It subsequently becomes clear that among the chattels brought away from the rectory were the valuable paintings that had graced its walls, and they remained with Sarah in her London homes.

In 1851, Thomas's occupation is given as 'army clothier', a contractor supplying clothing to the army. Some army clothiers became wealthy, among them John Jones (1800–82), who was born in London, but whose name sounds Welsh. Having served an apprenticeship as a tailor, in 1825 he established his own shop in the West End. He had begun collecting art as a young man and, as his business developed with army contracts and made him rich, he filled his house with paintings and art objects. He moved to larger premises and filled that, too. At the 1881 Census he was living at 95 Piccadilly, retired on 'income from dividends', with four servants. When he died on 7 January 1882, he left his collection to the South Kensington Museum (the V&A). John Jones and Sarah (before she married) shared a surname and, like John Jones, Sarah's son Thomas was an army clothier. What are we to make of these coincidences, to which one must add a common interest in collecting art? No matter how fervently I wish it, this further piece of circumstantial evidence is no proof of a link between her and John Jones of Piccadilly.

Then again, the drapery business runs like a bright thread through later episodes in the George and Sarah Williams story. Their daughter, Julia Frances, born 1797, married Evan Jones of Neath, a draper, on 21 March 1822. According to the Family Bible, he died in London on 14 December 1840, and that is why, in 1851, his widow was also living at 2 Cobourg Place, Hammersmith, with her mother. The paintings from the rectory came back to south Wales when Julia Sarah, daughter of Thomas, married Richard Jones (another Jones, another draper!) from Bridgend. There, at last, seventy years after they were first in jeopardy, the George Morlands and 'paintings by other distinguished painters', as we have already seen, were peremptorily and cheaply sold to assuage the anger of creditors. The circumstances are explained in the journal of David Jones:

> The son of this Richard Jones ... was in business with his father. In or about 1885 after some good agricultural sales and while they had some four thousands of pounds in their possession, the son bolted with all the money and got safe to America therewith, where he now is I suppose ... The father was left to bear the brunt of this evil deed. All his things were seized by the outraged creditors and sold.

It was at first puzzling that Richard Jones could have found himself in this predicament, but by 1861 he had done well enough to retire from the drapery business and within the next decade he had become an auctioneer and farmer. In 1881, he and his wife lived comfortably with three single daughters, all in their twenties, and two servants. Their son, George Edward, by then twenty-eight, had left home, but remained in business with his father as 'Richard Jones & Son', with offices at Bridgend Town Hall Chambers. In another four years or so he would rob his parents of their possessions, respect and peace of mind. Not unexpectedly, after this disaster, Julia Sarah and her husband left south Wales. In 1891, they were living with Ann Rosa, their youngest daughter, who was still unmarried, in Chorlton, Manchester, where Richard, farmer, auctioneer, man of affairs, was reduced to a 'coal dealer's traveller'. Ann Rosa, a 'fancy jeweller's assistant', was head of the household. Her parents died at the same address within weeks of one another in the winter of 1894–95, both aged sixty-nine.

Jones is all too common a surname in Wales and the plethora of Joneses in this story, while opening up all kinds of interesting possibilities to speculate upon, scuttles any hope of a satisfactory solution to my problem. As I have already mentioned, I have long supposed that our family's link with Merthyr Mawr was through Sarah Jones, wife of the Reverend George Williams, because she shares a surname with Thomas,

Ann and Stephen Jones who were the owners of that property before, mortgaged to the hilt, it fell like a ripe plum into the hands of Sir John Nicholl. But I should, perhaps, consider that the connection is not through Sarah, but through Richard Jones, husband of her granddaughter, Julia Sarah. There is the remote possibility that Richard Jones, draper, of Bridgend and John Jones, the wealthy army clothier, of London, are related. After all, the former met his wife-to-be in London, not south Wales.

Yet I could have been right all along. It is also just possible that Sarah Jones was of a family from Llangan, as John Perkins' diary suggests. Richard Jones was born in Colwinston, not far from Llangan across the 'Golden Mile', as that part of the A48 between Bridgend and Cardiff has long been known because of its extraordinary value as a toll road. I have read somewhere that the Joneses who inherited Merthyr Mawr from Charles Bowen were a Bridgend family. Who is to say that Sarah Jones and Richard Jones – and John Jones, the art collector – do not all have places on the same family tree?

Five

I THINK NOW of our children at the age of twelve and, more recently, our grandchildren, on their way to school, and how very young they were even for the trials of that experience. I cannot imagine them trudging off to a seven-and-a-half hour shift underground. And yet that was the fate of many of my ancestors and untold thousands born and brought up in the south Wales coalfield.

As much family history as I have been able to compile comes from census records and luckily surviving family documents, and from one unique source, the diary of a gentleman farmer in the Vale of Glamorgan preserved at the National Folk Museum in St Fagans. Oral history also plays a part in the form of stories of a grander past that my parents told me – which their parents had told them and so on. They stretch into the eighteenth century and beyond; stories that are unreliable, like Chinese whispers, as must always be the case with oral history. Despite my best efforts they are beyond proof, a certain amount of circumstantial evidence notwithstanding. The histories of the Adamses from the English Midlands, the Williamses of the Vale of Glamorgan, the Lewises from west Wales and the Loves of Somerset – rather like the tendrils of climbing plants that circle in the air seeking a hold to cling to and send out fresh leaves and blossoms for a while – converged in Gilfach Goch. Coal was the only reason for this convergence.

The story of my mother's family is somewhat different from that of my father, but all came seeking a livelihood and a home. Gilfach was not the first place they had tried, but it held out hope. The Williamses and Adamses were already there in 1881 and in the mid-1890s would have observed with considerable satisfaction that Christmas Evans, son of the pioneer who gave his name to Evanstown, was sinking two deep shafts at the top end of the valley. Given peace between workers and owners, employment would be secure for years to come. No need to move again. One of the pits, the Britannic, kept its promise: in 1923 it still employed more than 1,000 men, and it became the last in the valley to close in 1960. Raising their eyes above the dust and smoke of the valley floor, my people would have felt the green pocket of the valley enfold them, giving them a sense of a particular habitation to which they could belong.

Until my generation – and I was born in 1934 – all the men, both my grandfathers, and their fathers and their fathers before them so far as I can tell, spent their entire working lives in coal mines. Before that, in the eighteenth century, with the rare exception, they presumably laboured on the land. I know my paternal grandfather and namesake began working underground as a 'helper' with his father at the age of twelve. And what would have greeted him hundreds of feet below the surface? We have all seen photographs of colliers at the coalface. They show a coal seam as a black wall glinting back the light of lamps within the confines of the photographic frame. But of course, as a geologist would instantly point out, the apparently room-sized wall-like seam is a minute section through a layer of coal varying in thickness from inches to several feet spread over many square miles between similar enormous blankets of other rock formations laid down as sedimentary deposits millions of years ago. The identical coal seams were reached and pillaged by scores of collieries in different valleys and villages in the heyday of mining, and billions of tons of coal remain untapped now the collieries have all gone. In those old deep mines the coalface could be a hundred yards long or more, divided into 'stents' or 'stalls' of about twenty yards to be worked by individual colliers, some with helpers, and the network of tunnels to reach the coal and transport it to the surface could extend for many miles.

My father's reluctance to talk about his daily toil, and my own failure to ask him about it, left me without even a hazy second-hand impression of what it was like to the eyes; in the ears; on the lips, the tongue and skin; grasped by fingers and palms; under foot; along the muscles of the back and arms and thighs. I have read histories of the coalfield, but they are concerned with the broad sweep of events and the social consequences, often bad enough, goodness knows. Only in rare books like *These Poor Hands* by B. L. Coombes can you begin to feel the grit of it. Not long ago I talked with Vernon Harding, whose coal-grimed face appears in that famous Magnum photograph 'Three Generations of Miners', taken in 1950 by the eminent American photographer W. Eugene Smith. At eighty-six he is one of a small band of men still surviving who worked underground before mechanisation changed dramatically the way coal is extracted, before the introduction of steel roof supports, before conveyor belts carried the coal away from the face, before the coal cutters that my father knew – all too well. Vernon's account of his work as a helper alongside his father in Coedely Colliery at the age of fourteen in 1942 is the nearest I can reach to my grandfather's experience at the age of twelve.

Colliers were paid by the weight of coal cut and delivered to the weighbridge in individually marked drams, each designed to hold a ton, but by careful packing often containing half a ton more. Vernon's widowed father, determined to make the most of each working day, was invariably in the first 'bond' of men in the cage for the 6 a.m. descent – five hundred yards vertically down and then a mile walk cushioned by inches of coal dust along a tunnel cut to accommodate the width and height of a dram. There were no footpaths underground. If you happened to be in this tunnel when a horse-drawn journey of drams came clattering through, you crouched in the nearest 'manhole' niche in the side wall until it had passed. This was the main heading, the route to the coalface, off which turns were cut into the seam, and, as necessary, the layers of rock above and beneath it.

The No. 3 seam where Vernon and his father worked varied in thickness from eighteen to thirty inches. The first task was to create a space six feet wide and five feet deep where a dram could be placed on rails laid back to the main heading. This entailed boring holes and placing charges to break up the layer of rock beneath the seam, which in that place was less hard than the rock above, and then clearing away the rubble. The roof was supported by timber props notched and shaped at the ends with axes to make a jointed structure of pillars and cross beams. Apart from setting the explosive and blowing the rock, which was done by a shotsman on the night shift, all these preliminaries were the work of the miner, who had to drill the holes, complete the excavation, build the roof support and lay the rails, measuring crucial distances. The tools he used were his own, paid for, and at the end of a shift their handles were threaded onto an iron bar locked with his own padlock.

At the face Vernon's father had a safety lamp; he trimmed the wick and filled it with oil to give the light he worked by. Lying on one shoulder, he used a short handled pick to hack a slot six to nine inches deep in the rock along the base of the seam over a distance of about eight yards and then a longer handled mandrel to strike down the loosened coal. The fourteen-year-old's electric lamp with its heavy battery (which of course my grandfather did not have) was hung from a post behind him, so that he could see little of what lay in his shadow before him. His job was to scoop the fallen coal with bare hands and forearms into a steel curling box, and crawling, his back scraping the low roof, tug or slide this hundredweight container several yards back to the waiting dram. As the face moved forward stony waste was cast into the space behind, the gob, where a wall had first to be built to retain it. When the roof supports along the gob were removed, the rock layers above weighed down and sealed the man-made wound. During the shift you ate your meagre snap when there was a moment's pause at the stall you were working, as when a loaded dram was hauled away; sometimes there was no pause. You drank water from a quart tinplate jack to lay thirst and the constant dust, which you lived in, breathed and swallowed seven and a half hours each working day. The mine was ventilated by air driven by a fan at the head of one (downcast) shaft through a system of brattice-covered doors that directed the flow where it was needed and up another (upcast) shaft, but it was warm and had the fustiness of coal on it. To the warmth of the mine was added the heat of intense physical effort. Men worked stripped to the waist and their bodies were painted with sweat and black dust. The No. 3 seam was dry; many were wet and workable only by constant pumping.

In addition to physical strength, miners needed an array of skills not easily or quickly learned – for example, that of notching the ends of pit props precisely using a hatchet with a keen nine-inch blade, so that no time was wasted dismembering a roof support to adjust an ill-fitting joint. Vernon Harding was an apt learner, and his father a patient teacher, but it was five years before he was considered competent to have his own working place. Miners also needed constant wariness. The experienced man could detect weakness in the roof above by the sound returned when it was tapped with a mandrel handle, but you could never be certain. I remember my father telling me how a collier in the Squint had been killed when 'a stone fell on him'. It was a characteristic understatement: a stone might weigh many hundredweight, or have an edge sharp enough to sever a limb. And there were other dangers – from asphyxiating and explosive gas, bolting horses, runaway journeys, falling cages, and at the end, the long, slow death of coal dust in the lungs.

A colliery was almost a small town. Coedely in Vernon Harding's time employed well over 800 men, had a blacksmith's shop, a sawmill, brickworks, coke ovens and – towering above it on the hillside – its own landmark visible for miles, an enormous conical slag heap. As he wrote to me, 'The noise was always there – the grating chatter of the steel plates in the screens as they sorted the coal, the clang of buffers as the shunting loco moved trucks along the sidings, the rhythmic thump of the steam engines as the winders raised the cages, and the blast of hooters signalling the beginning and end of shifts.' There was also the omnipresent black dust, carried by the westerlies across the valley to terraced houses on the other side.

The terraces of Gilfach Goch were built because of the colliery, to which the lives of wives and mothers were as dedicated as those of their husbands and sons. It was a village community with a single focus, replete with mutual understanding and sympathy, whose families shared alike occasional blessings and years of adversity. Scores of towns and villages much the same lined the valleys of the south Wales coalfield. The settlements are still there, but the sense of purpose and solidarity that animated them as communities all but died with the closure of the mines. In George Yates's 1799 map of the county of Glamorgan, Cardiff is an insignificant burg with a quay on the estuary of the Taff and Barry barely exists. Some growth and industry is emerging around Swansea, Merthyr is beginning to burgeon, and a little activity is occurring in the Cynon Valley. But the Rhondda and adjacent valleys to west and east are virtually empty. Without coal they would all still be empty. Furthermore, without coal, our populous coastal urban areas, most notably Cardiff-Penarth-Barry, would more than likely have only a fraction of their current population and importance. The working of iron and other metal ores was highly significant, but Welsh coal was crucial to industrial and mercantile development here and elsewhere in the UK. Coal created modern south Wales. As I write, the Assembly government is planning a memorial to mining disasters in which more than five men were killed, some 200 of them. It will be sited at Senghenydd, near Caerffili, where on the morning of 14 October 1913, an explosion at the Universal Colliery killed 439 men and boys. It is long overdue – and it is not enough. What is needed is a memorial to Vernon Harding and tens of thousands like him who worked in the hundreds of collieries that dotted the coalfield, and to the women who shared their lives: a grand memorial to coal, without which south Wales would be largely an extension of the green desert that is mid-Wales.

Six

With the story of Bloom, the first surviving child of the Reverend George and Sarah, and his children I am on firmer ground, and the scene shifts from the Vale, London and the wider world to the Valleys, from agriculture in one form or another to coal mining.

Bloom Williams, who was about twenty-five at the time of his father's death, gave the remainder of his life to farming. He probably found a holding, or employment on the land, in Llysworney, some seven miles west of Llantrithyd, soon after his father died, for on 2 May 1816 he married Mary Thomas of that place. The birthplaces of their children, recorded in the Family Bible, disclose a life lived among the villages of the Vale, including Pickett near Llandow; a farm, Penalan (presumably Penylan) in the parish of Coychurch, near Bridgend; Court Lamphey (now Llampha Court); and Mount Pleasant. The longest period of residence, at least nine years, seems to have been at Court Lamphey, a substantial farmhouse with a barn range up a long lane in Colwinston, also the home village of Richard Jones, successful draper and later ruined auctioneer of Bridgend.

Four of the children of Bloom and Mary died in infancy and there was one stillbirth, but in 1841 the parents and four surviving children were living in the hamlet of Mount Pleasant. Bloom's occupation was formally recorded as 'agricultural labourer', and possibly he was never any more than that. Ten years later he declared he was a shepherd and the family were living at Pentwyn, Pencoed, not far from Penylan, the farm where, in 1819, Frances Sarah, their second child, was born, and again in the parish of Coychurch, which was also Bloom's birthplace. In 1861 they were in the same parish, but at a new address, Penprysk Road. Bloom, still employed, was seventy and his wife sixty-five; their son, William, aged twenty-seven, also an agricultural labourer, lived with them.

The Family Bible records the death of Mary, on 4 July 1863. Widower Bloom, aged eighty, claimed to be still at work in 1871. In the 'Occupation' column the census enumerator first entered 'formerly gardener', and then, in response, one imagines, to strong demur, deleted 'formerly'. William still shared a home with his father, but his circumstances had changed. He had married Mary Isaac in late spring or early summer of 1865. She was the daughter of James and Margaret Isaac, born (as the Family Bible testifies) 12 December 1840, at Llanwrda near Llandovery, Carmarthenshire. She was unquestionably Welsh-speaking, and whether or not her husband was in some degree Welsh-speaking, had a strong influence on the language of the home. William was no longer an agricultural labourer; he was a collier. Within the next decade he, his wife and their growing family moved to Gilfach Goch. To that change of job and home I owe my existence.

***

The second legend I heard as a child comes from Dats's family. It claims an ancestor was once Lord Mayor of London. There was, indeed, a Thomas Adams, born 1586, who became Lord Mayor of London in 1654–55. This Thomas Adams, from Wem in Shropshire, became a draper in London and eventually Master of the Drapers' Company. A staunch royalist, he was knighted by Charles II at The Hague and created baronet soon after. He was a notable philanthropist: he endowed a free school at Wem, which was housed in his former home, founded an Arabic professorship at Cambridge, paid for the translation and printing of the Gospels in Persian and left legacies to aid hospitals and the poor of several parishes. He died, full of years, in 1668, at his country estate in Sprowston, Norfolk, and is memorialised in the church there.

Dats's father, the Thomas Adams to whom I am certainly related, was born at Great Bridge, Staffordshire, on the border of West Bromwich, and now swallowed up in the metropolitan area of Birmingham. And *his* father, William, was from Newhall in south Derbyshire. Great Bridge is some forty miles south-east of Wem, Newhall perhaps twenty-five miles further east. Both are, as I discovered in researching later generations of the Adams family (who moved often in pursuit of work), in reasonable proximity for there to have been, five or more generations back, a connection with the man who became Lord Mayor of London. If there is a distant kinship, I have found it incapable of proof. Yet, as with the Merthyr Mawr story, there is a link, surely, however tenuous.

Thomas Adams, my great-grandfather, was a pit-sinker, a calling in demand in south Wales in the nineteenth century. He was illiterate; what could he know of the Civil War and the Restoration? How might he have learned of a namesake who, 200 years before, was Lord Mayor of London? How could he have claimed a connection, if he was not indeed related, however remotely, and had received this information, as I did, from parents?

My father told me nothing I can recall about his family life while he was growing up. The problem, I suspect, is that I was lamentably poor at asking questions he might well have been happy to answer. Now it is much too late. In place of his narrative and insights, census returns at ten-year intervals supplemented by those documents that have survived must serve my purpose. I know that mining brought Mam and Dats together, because, from different directions, their parents and grandparents came to make a home and a living where collieries and ironworks promised steady wages.

As previously mentioned, William Adams, Dats's grandfather came from Newhall, a village in south Derbyshire, where mining began on a large scale in the late eighteenth century. He had probably married Rachel, who was born at Llangynidr, Breconshire, about 1826, for their first child, Ann, was born in 1827. I cannot say where William and Rachel met and married, but would hazard a guess it was in or near Blaenafon, Monmouthshire, where coal mining and iron working began in the 1780s and was well established by the 1820s.

In 1841 the family was living in Cwmdu, now part of Maesteg in the Llynfi Valley. Coal and iron reserves in the area were exploited from the 1820s, one of the companies involved being the Cambrian Iron and Spelter Co., which gave its name to the street where William and Rachel lived with their children and two lodgers. Catherine, a baby aged four months, was born there. Apart from Ann and one further exception, the others – Elizabeth, Solomon, Samuel, Rachel and Sarah, whose ages ranged from nine to two years – were all born at Abersychan, Monmouthshire. The exception was Thomas, the oldest boy, aged thirteen in 1841, born at Great Bridge, Staffordshire, who would become Dats's father.

The number of times William and Rachel moved house, with six or more children, all their furniture and belongings, by horse-drawn cart or wagon, amazes me. Starting, let us suppose, in Abersychan, where they may have been for two or three years in the early 1820s, they travelled north to Staffordshire for four years or so, back again to Abersychan for seven years, then to Cwmdu for four years, and back once more to Abersychan. There in 1851 the three older sons, Thomas, Solomon and Samuel, were working alongside their father as pit-sinkers and iron stone miners. With four wages coming in, perhaps Rachel could at last feel the family was comfortably off.

On Christmas Eve 1856, Thomas married Hannah Evans, who came from Rhymni, Glamorganshire, at the parish church in Llanhilleth. I have their marriage certificate. It is grimy, as though often handled by someone with coal dust ingrained in the whorls of his finger ends, and missing the right hand quarter – probably because, when I was young I lusted after the Queen Victoria stamp that was affixed there. Bride and groom signed with a cross. In 1861 the couple and their daughter Ruth, aged two, were living at Queen Street, Blaina. Thomas Adams was a pit-sinker in 1861, as he had been at the time of his marriage five years before. His particular skills lay in driving shafts and headings through rock to reach the coal seams.

By 1871, as we have seen, Thomas and Hannah's home was in Ogmore Vale. There were five children, four of whom had been born in Abersychan. The lone exception was Samuel, then aged two, who would become my grandfather, and first saw light in Llanharan, in the Vale of Glamorgan. During the next decade they moved again, to 9 Talbot Terrace, Gilfach Goch, at the very top of the valley. By 1881, Hannah had given birth to another three sons – George, John and Thomas – and Samuel, now twelve, was working with their father in the pit as a miner's help like his older brother William. To obtain release from school at that age he would have passed a test of competence in reading and writing, though the standard normally required was not high.

After the years of movement among the valleys of the coalfield, Thomas and Hannah Adams found in Gilfach Goch a place where they were content to settle. In that same year, 1881, the expanded Williams family was also living at the top of Gilfach valley, in a terrace known as Rose Hill Cottages. Margaret, who would become my grandmother, was not entered on the census form, but her younger sisters, Anne, Elizabeth, Amelia and Julia were there, together with Octavius, not yet one, who would die early the following year. He was the second of the sons of William and Mary to die in infancy. It was not altogether surprising; a child needed to be hardy and blessed by fortune to survive. Records show that in 1881 there was 'not a yard of sewer in the whole [of Gilfach Goch]' and sanitary arrangements were 'of a rudimentary character'. A serious outbreak of typhoid fever in the spring of 1886 may account for the death of one-year-old William James Williams on 25 June that year. It was not until January 1905 that houses were connected to a water supply.

Rose Hill Cottages were not far from Talbot Terrace, where the Adamses lived. William Williams worked underground in the same pit as Thomas Adams and his sons. The families almost certainly knew one another. In any event, Samuel Adams met and came to know Margaret Williams. Their acquaintance grew to friendship, friendship to love. When they married on 19 January 1891, at Sardis (Independents') Chapel, Pontypridd, both aged twenty-two, they signed the certificate with neat cursive hands. Thomas Adams, the groom's father, had died in the summer of 1887, but William Williams was present to give his daughter away. The couple's first home was next door to Margaret's parents.

William Williams died at Rose Hill Cottages on 4 April 1916, in the second year of the Great War, aged eighty-three. At Coychurch, in the grave he shares with Mary and three children who died in infancy in Gilfach Goch, the memorial stone says he was eighty-eight when he died. Perhaps it was Mary's best guess, because he had declared his age and date of birth inaccurately at every census since 1871. In 1901 he said he was born in 1841 and aged sixty, when he was actually almost sixty-nine – and still working as a labourer on the colliery surface. Whereas the earlier inaccuracies of two or three years may have been slips, this appears an attempt to disguise his true age, though for what purpose it is impossible to guess. Perhaps it was carelessness, or mischief, cocking a snook at officialdom. In 1891, asked about the language of the family, he said they spoke Welsh only, which was also a fib. He died intestate and Letters of Administration (part of the hoard I had stored in plastic bags) were granted to his widow – as the official note attached to the document states:

'upon the condition that no portion of the assets shall be distributed or paid during the War to any beneficiary or creditor who is a German, Austro-Hungarian, Turkish or Bulgarian subject'.

His estate was valued at £195 and 18 shillings. Mary

Williams died on 20 February 1918. She was seventy-three. No formal document exists mentioning a will, or probate, or letters of administration. Instead, on a foolscap ledger sheet, 'the actual account of estate' of the deceased is neatly detailed by an unknown, un-legalistic hand. Mary had £150 savings at the Post Office, and there were various debts outstanding, including a loan to Samuel Adams of £20. Among the expenses were 2s 1d for telegrams sent to relations, and train and cab fares amounting to 13s 3d. Extra groceries to provide for family and friends cost £1 12s 7d. The funeral furnishers were paid £20 9s. When she joined William in the grave close to the church porch in Coychurch, refreshments for the mourners were provided at the White Horse, a pub directly across the road from the graveyard, at a cost of £4 19s. After deduction of these expenses, the remaining £184 14s was equally divided among Mary's six daughters, my grandmother, Margaret, and my great aunts, Sarah, Annie, Elizabeth, Amelia and Julia Elizabeth. Although Sarah is the only one with a literary connection (of sorts – the poet Huw Menai was a lodger in her home while he lived in Gilfach), I am ashamed to say my Aunty Lizzie is the only one with whom I had any acquaintance. It was to her house near the top of the valley, a short stone's throw from the Trane Colliery, that my father and I would trudge on Christmas mornings, once, memorably, along a path cut through snow almost waist high. Although a teetotaller, she would insist we had a little drink and hand us breakfast cups filled with 'medicinal' whisky. I remember her tenderly: an aged woman, with a pale face and blue eyes watery behind steel-rimmed spectacles, dressed in black, and perfectly pear-shaped. She was so small I had to bend low to kiss her wrinkled cheek when we said goodbye. Tom Roberts, her husband, who had come south to the mines from Corwen in north Wales, had died of appendicitis in his thirties, leaving her to bring up eight children by her own humble labours, washing and cleaning for others. They worshipped her. Two of the sons, in middle age, still lived at home: these were my Roberts cousins who drove the St John Ambulance that served the valley.

Seven

HISTORIANS GWYN ALF Williams and Dai Smith refer to the 'shopocracy' of Merthyr Tydfil and the Rhondda townships – that body of shopkeepers who well knew their commercial success and personal prosperity were dependent upon good order in the community they served. They were generally wealthier than their customers and, remarkably, had a life expectancy twice as long. They wanted nothing more than to see workers employed in regular labour with regular wages to spend – with good reason. In the troubles of 1911, individual shopkeepers reported drops in takings of between £65 and £160 a week. Strikes, lockouts, recession, unemployment – no matter what the cause – were anathema to them. As informal (sometimes secretive) groups or, in the twentieth century, organised chambers of trade, they sought to bring influence to bear on local councils and the population at large to restore and maintain calm, sobriety and normal conditions.

I am not sure anything like an organised shopkeeper voice ever emerged in Gilfach Goch, where there were few shops because the valley had a small population. This was especially the case before the construction of the City, which began just before the First World War and continued after it, brought a fresh influx of people. Even if shopkeepers had been inclined to present a common front and appeal to authority about the desperate need for road improvements, for example, how could they hope to succeed when the administration of such matters resided with three local councils habituated to non-cooperation?

The shops I came to know in the early 1940s were dominated by the multi-departmental Co-op in High Street, at the T-junction barely fifty yards from home, which supplied almost all our daily needs. With the possible exception of Pegler's, one of a chain of south Wales grocery stores, every one of the Co-op's departments – grocer's, butcher's, footwear, hardware, drapery, dispensing chemist – was bigger than any other shop in the valley. It also supplied milk door-to-door from a grand horse-drawn wagon, for which customers paid with small metal milk tokens, known as Co-op checks. These were obtained from the half-glazed box between grocery and footwear where members' Co-op books were made up, accounts settled and dividends calculated. The Co-op was the commercial hub of the village, an institution, and as is the way in retail trade other businesses gathered close by. Evanstown had a few shops, notably Thomas and Evans's grocery. Rather more served the top of the valley, including Lewis Jenkins's double-fronted store, one broad window fronting the butcher's and the other the grocery shop, and the trading post from which the Griffiths family sent forth horse-drawn carts laden with fruit and vegetables and, on Fridays, fish, cockles and laverbread. The City, too, had its cluster at a crossroads, dominated by an Italian corner shop that belonged at first to the Tambini family, with whom my grandfather was particularly friendly.

The Co-op did not exist when my thrifty grandfather began to think of starting a business, but commercial premises were already concentrated to the east of the Ogwr Fach in High Street, the long main road to the upper reaches of the valley. Although the beginnings of community seem to have been in Evanstown, in 1912, according to the *Wales Trades Directory*, it had only three shops, one of which, in Abercerdin Road, was the sole 'house furnishers' in Gilfach. Of the remaining twenty-six shops, twenty-one were in High Street, including four bootmakers, two confectioners, two drapers, three grocers, a chemist and pharmacist, a fruiterer and greengrocer, a hairdresser, two 'general dealers' and four butchers. This may not appear to add up, but two of the butchers were also grocers. The one fried fish shop, in Evanstown, also sold confectionery, and another confectioner's, in Gelliarael Road, was the first shop a visitor journeying up the valley would come across. The fried fish shop in Abercerdin Road offered a pioneering line in convenience food, and the well-scattered confectioners catered for the sweet-toothed, but there was little to supply the needs of those setting up home, still less to tempt rash expenditure on trifles and finery. It is hard to imagine the lone hairdresser's repertoire of skills extending further than a short back and sides. For those who could afford them, Gilfach shops provided the necessities of life, nothing more.

But there were shops in Tonypandy and Penygraig, which for a population concentrated in the upper part of Gilfach Goch (before the construction of the City) and lacking regular public transport, were closer and grander than those in Tonyrefail. A well-worn path over the mountain is clearly visible in old photographs of the top of the valley. It is certainly a steep climb either side of the watershed between the Ogwr Fach and Nant Clydach, but not far across the top, and miners on either side were well used to it when, for whatever reason, there was no work for them in local pits.

Most of the pedestrian traffic was from Gilfach via Clydach Vale to the Rhondda, where there were many collieries and many more, and more varied, businesses. At the turn of the century, besides a plethora of stores offering foods and drapery of one kind and another, Tonypandy had a bookseller and stationer; a cabinet maker and upholsterer; a firm of carpenters, joiners and builders; and one of painters, glaziers and paperhangers; two ironmongers; a woman who dealt in glassware and china; two watchmakers and jewellers – and three hairdressers. Those who ventured a little farther down the Rhondda to Penygraig would find two more booksellers and stationers, a furniture broker, a 'fancy repository' and, before the trudge home, a restorative 'eating house'.

The predominance of grocery stores is understandable. Men and boys employed in gruelling hard labour every working day needed sustenance. The emphasis on food in the pages of *How Green Was My Valley* is not misplaced, even if it is laid on in paradisal quantities. Rhys Davies's description in *Print of a Hare's Foot* of Blaenclydach's rather grand Royal Stores – where, at first, his family lived above the shop – is nearer to the visual and olfactory experience of my childhood (and a world away from our refrigerated supermarkets):

> There were lettered canisters of black and gold, an odorous coffee-grinding machine, mounds of yellow Canadian and pallid Caerphilly cheeses, rosy cuts of ham and bacon, wide slabs of butter cut by wire for the scales, and bladders of lard. Behind the counter over which my mother presided, stretched wall-fixtures stacked with crimson packets of tea, blue satchels of sugar, vari-coloured bags of rice, dried fruits and peas [...] Soaps gave their own clean smell [...] Slabs of rich cake lay in a glass case on an intersecting counter stacked with biscuit tins. Packets of Ringer's tobacco, black chewing shag, spices, almonds and dried herbs occupied a row of drawers under a counter ...

While work was plentiful and uninterrupted by industrial conflict, customers paid their bills and grocers flourished, but there were few prolonged periods of prosperity in the south Wales coalfield. The 1926 strike and the years of the Depression that followed hard upon it, desperate for the unemployed, were not a great deal better for the Valleys grocer. Idris Davies encapsulates the situation in a micro-drama:

> Mrs Evans fach, you want butter again.
> How will you pay for it now, little woman
> With your husband out on strike, and full
> Of the fiery language? Ay, I know him,
> His head is full of fire and brimstone
> And a lot of palaver about communism,
> And me, little Dan the Grocer
> Depending so much on private enterprise.

When my grandfather went into business he was possibly

prompted by the example of Lewis Jenkins, the butcher and grocer, whose fine shop was just across the road in the upper part of High Street. The families were close and, quite soon, connected by marriage. Inspired he may have been, but he was not a risk taker, there was no question of giving up his job in the pit to become a shopkeeper. He also saw there was little point in setting up as a rival to a successful grocery shop, virtually on its doorstep. But there was an opening for a supplier of furniture and household goods in that populous part of Gilfach, where the alternatives were in Evanstown or Tonypandy, and that's what my grandfather, a collier like his neighbours, seized upon, and made a modest success of, alongside his work in the pit. A few years later everyone who could afford it wanted electric light, and with a son who was an electrician, Sam Adams had the answer to that, too.

Eight

As ALREADY MENTIONED, at the 1891 Census, William Williams and Mary, and their daughters Amelia and Julia declared they spoke Welsh only. Next door, Samuel and Margaret Adams, as yet childless, for they had married only three months before, spoke Welsh and English. My grandparents had two children while they lived at Rose Hill Cottages, Elizabeth Julia, who was born in 1892, and Bloom, born in 1894. They moved in 1896 or 1897 to a house about a half-mile farther down the valley in what was then called Sherwood Terrace. My confidence about the date of the move comes from the naming of my father, who was born in 1897: he was Thomas Sherwood Adams, because his was the first birth registered in the terrace. The address no longer exists – like several other blocks of housing bearing different names in a 1900 map of Gilfach, it was later incorporated into High Street.

Sherwood, I surmise, was the name, or perhaps the whim, of the builder. Why Mam and Dats gave it to their baby son is a more difficult question. They may have thought it somehow enhanced his chances in life, rather as Trismegistus was supposed to guarantee good fortune to the child misnamed Tristram Shandy. For the time and place it is an outlandish name, though in keeping with the way the language of the area was changing. Whereas the parents were bilingual, at the 1901 Census their three children were said to speak English only. By 1911, however, Bloom, who was seventeen and still at school, was recorded as speaking both Welsh and English, which suggests a good deal of Welsh persisted in the home.

In 1911 Samuel, Margaret and their three children were living at 165 High Street, which may be a re-designated address, as suggested above. A recent visit to Gilfach revealed a simple two-storey terraced house, in which, by what shifts of compression I cannot easily imagine, they contrived to afford a spare room. This allowed them to boost the family income by taking in lodgers – two assistant teachers, one of whom, Daniel Timothy Jenkins, a 'certificated teacher' from Llanfihangel Ystrad, Cardiganshire, became a friend of the family. The house, near the top of High Street, was not far from the premises where Lewis Jenkins had established his butcher's shop and grocery. Jenkins came from Coychurch, the same parish as Mam's father and it is possible they knew one another before arriving in Gilfach. In any event, fresh and stronger connections were made between the families in the 1900s. There would have been much to-and-fro-ing between the households, first because Tim, one of my grandparents' lodgers, married the Jenkins's daughter Louisa, and a little later their elder son, Bloom, married another daughter, Edith.

That their lodgers in 1911 were two teachers, and that they retained the friendship of one of them, suggests my grandparents kept a neat home and had a good deal of personal charm. But why did they take in lodgers, with the extra housework and the loss of living space within the family home it entailed? For the extra money, obviously. But I think there may have been a stronger imperative. I am reasonably confident that Dats was working at the Britannic Colliery. The sinking of the Trane might have been under way, but the pit was not operational, whereas the Brit was well established and productive – when the men were in work. In 1910, however, as part of the Cambrian Combine it was involved in that prolonged and bitter strike in which large numbers of police and military were deployed against the miners. I believe my grandparents took lodgers who would not be affected by the vicissitudes of the coal industry as insurance against sudden loss of income when the next strike came.

Formal head-and-shoulders portraits of Samuel and Margaret (actually large tinted photographs) in oval mounts and carved wooden frames, used to be on a landing wall upstairs in the house in Gilfach. Taken when they were young, perhaps in 1891, about the time they were married, they now hang in our hallway. They mean a great deal to me. My grandfather, head turned slightly to the right, handsome in young manhood, looks frankly out at you. His brown hair is neatly parted and he wears a dark suit. His white shirt collar is turned down over a bow tie, its floppy ends neatly concealed by the high-buttoned jacket. He is the image of self-possession. His new wife wears a plain black dress, buttoned to the throat, beneath which a hint of frilled white collar is visible. At her throat is a cameo brooch set in a gold mount from which hangs a braided gold chain. She looks to the right; her hair, very fair, perhaps sandy, is swept back so that it appears almost boyish. She has a short straight nose and a small chin; her lips are slightly parted. It is not easy to reconcile the formality of the portraits, the impression they give of calm prosperity, with his daily labour as a miner and hers as a miner's wife, soon to be mother of his children.

Another, equally formal studio photograph taken nine or ten years later has Dats in the role of paterfamilias, standing dark-suited, wing-collared, with waistcoat and watch chain. Julia, eldest of the three children, stands on his right. The two boys have dark suits and waistcoats like their father, but their trousers are knickerbockers and they have boots to be proud of. The older boy, Bloom, stands posed like a politician of the period, his right hand across his chest holding his open jacket just below the left lapel. Their mother is seated, her long, full skirt sweeping the floor. She wears an embroidered fitted jacket of the same material as the skirt, with high neck and puff sleeves, and has a very small waist. There is a glimpse of white blouse at the neck, where the round collar is fastened with a simple brooch, which I remember from my own childhood days – a narrow elongated oval, almost like a tie-pin, in gold of two or three colours. The younger boy sits on a stool, his right arm across his mother's knees. This is Tom, my father, no more than four years old and baby-faced still. In his left hand he holds a thin cane, possibly a riding switch, an unexpected accessory. All four look at the camera with no hint of a smile. Being photographed is a serious business: the father may be a 'hewer of coal', but they know how to dress for an occasion and have the clothes to make a show.

I know little of my father's brother and sister. I once spent a week in Llanelli with Aunty Julia – who was still then dark-haired, wore spectacles and was kind to me in a motherly way – and taciturn Uncle Will, a Cornishman, manager of the town's YMCA. Their daughter Jean was much the same age as my sisters and their son John a little older than me. John had been born profoundly deaf and, though anxious to communicate, could not speak. Jean cared deeply for him and, while she was present, John's frustration subsided and pleasure spread around us. Many years later, towards the end of her life, I began visiting Jean in Llanelli. She was the last link with that generation of my family and it is to her I owe some knowledge of Uncle Bloom. He qualified as a mining engineer and married Edith, daughter of Lewis Jenkins, the Gilfach Goch butcher and grocer. They had a pretty daughter called Molly, who was also about the same age as my sisters, and they lived in Gorseinon. My uncle's work had taken him to the Swansea Valley, and he became responsible for two collieries, at Penllergaer and Morlais. He must have been among the wealthier workers in the mining industry. I met him a few times. He was very different from my father, more out-going, even flamboyant. He bore a passing resemblance to Adolf Hitler, which at the time you might think he would do his utmost to disguise. But to the contrary, his natural cow's lick was allowed to fall across his forehead and he grew a moustache in the style of the Führer. I don't believe he was a fascist or an admirer of Hitler; I think he did it out of contrariness or devilment. When I passed the scholarship, he sent me a big, white £5 note, which I spent on a Timex wristwatch with a broad-sweep red second hand. I wore the watch to school and it soon broke. Jean told me Uncle Bloom was an alcoholic and when Edith hid his bottles he became violent and smashed the furniture. Found unconscious in the street and presumed drunk, he was put in a police cell to sleep it off. A doctor called to assess his condition recognised he was in a diabetic coma. This was a sharp warning: he forswore alcohol and maintained thereafter a strict diet, which included drinking glasses of cabbage-water. After the war, instead of employing an agent, Uncle Bloom expected his brother to keep an eye on the maintenance needs of houses in Coedely that had been left to him in Mam's will (of which more anon). There was otherwise little contact between them. I went with my father once to view the properties and saw he resented this imposition.

By 1911, my grandfather had been a collier working underground at the coalface for thirty years. Perhaps recognised as having more to offer than the vast experience he shared with many others, he had been noticed by the pit managers, for in the last image I have of him, dated 2 May 1914, he is in a group photograph of forty-eight 'Cambrian Colliery Officials, Gilfach Goch Section' on an outing to Mumbles on Swansea Bay. They are assembled in front of a café, where a convenient short flight of steps allows them to be posed in four rows. It is after lunch, perhaps. Wives or waitresses are watching from the windows behind. In the middle of the seated front row is a stout, side-whiskered gent, who may be the mine owner's principal agent. Dats is standing, the outermost figure on the right. He wears a suit and waistcoat, wing-collar and tie, as do most of the others, and has a moustache, another very common feature. He is clearly of no more than medium height.

By 1916, when he was negotiating the loan from William Llewellyn to buy 27 High Street, he was well established in the role of overman, or underground foreman, charged with ensuring safety and satisfactory working in his section of the pit. His distinctive brass safety lamp was a badge of office. I was told he sang hymns as he went about the mine, so that those toiling at the face knew he was on his way: he never came upon a man idling. His responsibilities demanded longer hours underground than the colliers, and returned more than double their wage. Even so, it is surely remarkable that he found £253 to settle the mortgage account with William Llewellyn in just two years. How did he accumulate such wealth, which cannot have been common in Gilfach Goch at the time?

Among the documents and papers I brought away from the house in Gilfach were bank passbooks belonging to my grandfather and scores of invoices and receipts dating from 1916 to 1940. The two slim, red Lloyds passbooks run continuously from December 1916 to March 1921. Perhaps there were others that have not survived, or perhaps, for whatever reason, the sequence of recorded transactions ended there. The business certainly went on. The passbooks are headed 'Mr Samuel Adams, Furniture Dealer, 165 High Street, Gilfach Goch' and list outgoing cleared cheques and moneys deposited on facing pages. It is not possible to say where all his business income came from, because these entries are classed as 'sundries', but the payees on cleared cheques are identified and sometimes recognisable. For instance, on 26 February 1916 there is the record of £86 paid to 'Llewellyn', the first instalment of mortgage repayment. Others follow until the final £147 on 3 August 1918, when the house at 27 High Street became finally and wholly my grandfather's property.

Payments to Bramwell Booth, General of the Salvation Army, throw light on the seriousness of my grandparents' commitment to that cause and, incidentally, on their business activity: £12 6s on 17 April 1917; £23 5s on 28 March 1918; £32 7s on 3 April 1919. The regularity of the payment dates suggests an annual tithe, and if a tenth of business income went each year to the Army, it is possible to calculate what that income was: £123 in the year ending April 1917, £232 the following year, and £324 in the next.

These were substantial sums equivalent to several thousands of pounds today.

His spare-time business was expanding, but I can only guess now how it was conducted. By 1916, my grandparents had acquired what had previously been The Parsonage, yet they retained 165 High Street as a business address – an ordinary terraced house, which so far as it is possible to tell never had a window where goods could be displayed, far less a storeroom for stock. The collection of invoices reveals that contacts were established with furniture warehouses and fancy goods suppliers, but how customers chose goods is unclear – unless they did so from catalogues. Two or more cheques were sent at different times to 'Leech', 'Ingersoll', 'Kerslakes', 'Barnett', 'Abrahams', and 'Simplex'. Ingersoll is the famous American watch manufacturer. Barnett and Abrahams (in bank clerk's shorthand) both refer to Barnett H. Abrahams Ltd of Hatton Garden, London, 'merchants, manufacturers and shippers' of a wide range of cutlery, clocks, watches, jewellery and so on, a company that finally expired in 1974. Simplex, now a giant American manufacturing company, was founded in 1899 and still produces tools and electrical goods. Nothing can be made of the others.

The company name that appears most often in the Lloyds passbooks is GEC, the General Electric Company Ltd. My grandfather sent them twenty-five cheques in five business years for a total of £311 15s 5d, making GEC by far his most important supplier. GEC was established in the 1880s and produced the first electrical parts catalogue in 1887. It developed the use of china as an insulating material in switches, manufactured light bulbs from 1893 and also made telephones, electric bells and ceiling roses. (When our kitchen here was refurbished in 2009, the old fuse box containing ceramic fuses strung with wire of varying grades, probably manufactured by GEC a century ago, was finally replaced.) A further question follows: what use was made of all the electrical equipment my grandfather bought? A single surviving invoice carrying a brightly coloured advertisement for Osram Lamps, but with the printed heading 'Bought of S. ADAMS, Electrical Fitter, HIGH STREET, GILFACH GOCH' explains his investment. It is dated 13 July 1918 and has been used to record not a sale but the purchase of yet more electrical goods from 'A. Arthur' by Tom Adams – my father.

At the census on 2 April 1911, my father was within a couple of months of his fourteenth birthday. He had already left school, perhaps at the beginning of the Easter holiday, and had a job, as 'assistant baker'. I believe I see his parents discussing how to keep him out of the colliery and yet with a trade and assured employment. They knew William Furnival, a neighbour in Sherwood Terrace, who had left the colliery to start in business as a baker. No doubt it seemed a good first step in employment for their youngest. How long this career lasted I cannot tell, but I suspect it was brief, for neither my father nor my mother ever mentioned it. He may not have had an aptitude for school learning like his brother Bloom, the mining engineer, but he had an intuitive empathy with machines of all kinds. Two cheques recorded in the passbooks refer to 'autocycle', and I am confident the vehicle was his, because he had a passion for motorbikes.

I remember my father telling me (or perhaps it was my mother) that he installed electricity in many of the houses in our part of Gilfach Goch. Where he learned electrical fitting is a mystery. In all likelihood his skills were acquired on the job, because he had no formal qualifications for the work. Those handsomely-bound volumes of *Electrical and Mechanical Engineering* in the right hand cupboard of the big, mirror-topped sideboard were obviously intended as a self-instruction manual towards qualification. They were in pristine condition on the day when my sisters and I, emptying the sideboard of its contents, added them to the pile to be thrown out. Since the passbooks record all income as sundries, my father's contribution to the business is unknowable, but it may well have been substantial. He also worked as electrician in the colliery, a job that would have given him exemption from conscription in the First World War.

***

At this point a man named Bravo, a bogeyman of my childhood, enters the story. He robbed my grandfather. This might seem the kind of traumatic event that would be remembered in every detail by my parents and, in turn, passed on to me, but it was not. All I know is that Bravo was a thief, and that he ran away, leaving his wife and a daughter behind in Gilfach where, given the circumstances, they might have been victimised. Instead, they were looked after by my grandparents.

I don't know when the robbery occurred, but such evidence as I have suggests it was probably in the early 1930s, because my sisters and my cousin Jean (all three born between 1921 and 1924) remembered Freda, the Bravos' daughter. I have a photograph of my sisters with Freda. She has abundant curly, black hair and wears a pale, floral print dress. Joan appears to be about five, Freda at least five years older. Jean told me that Mrs Bravo and Freda, during the period of their abandonment, spent some time with her mother and father in Port Talbot, Aunty Julia and Uncle Will having moved there (she said) in 1931. The late date of these events appears to be confirmed by a witty, undated postcard to my parents from Uncle Bloom in Gorseinon: 'Mam and Mrs Bravo are returning to their Gilfach Goch residence tomorrow. Please bring the Rolls Royce. You need not wear your uniform, they are travelling "Incognito".'

The 'Rolls Royce' was my father's motorbike and sidecar, but the really intriguing feature of the card is the red penny George V stamp, which is of a design introduced in 1934. Mam and Mrs Bravo were clearly close friends and the words 'returning to their residence' suggest they resided at the same address, which can only have been our family home. Mother and daughter, then, lived with my grandparents while they waited for news and help from elsewhere.

Freda's birth certificate, dated February 1917, told me her father's forename was Harris, and that he was married to Amelia, whose maiden name was Bletcher. More recently I discovered that Harris was a common adaptation of the Yiddish Hershel, so perhaps that was the name his parents gave him. *Beit Hatfutsot* – the Museum of the Jewish People – cannot find the family name Bravo on its database. Presumably that too was adopted when the family came to Britain, though perhaps they picked it up en route in Italy, for it is an Italian name. At the 1901 Census, Bravo, his wife and three small children were living near the top of High Street, not far from Sherwood Terrace where my grandparents lived at the time. When asked where they were born, both Harris and Amelia replied 'Russia'. In 1911 they added that their nationality was 'Hebrew'. It seems likely they were among those families that fled westwards in the early 1880s during the anti-Jewish pogroms that swept south-west Russia (present-day Ukraine and Poland), following the assassination of Tsar Alexander II. Perhaps after initially settling with their kin in the East End of London, Hershel and Amelia (or Milly) married and came to south Wales in search of a job and security. My sisters told me Bravo came from London; they didn't know his birthplace was much farther east.

In Gilfach, he was a 'haulier underground', that is, he worked with the pit horses. My grandfather's younger brothers, George, John and Thomas, who were also hauliers, would have known him well. It is almost certain that Harris and Amelia married not long before they settled in Gilfach and at the 1911 Census they had seven children, all born in the valley. But they no longer lived there: within the previous two years or so they had moved to Gilfach Bargoed, in Cwm Rhymni, which was where Freda, their last child, was born. Harris was then employed as a steelworks labourer, and he probably remained a steelworker until the war and conscription ended. In the late 1920s, with Milly and Freda (the older children having left home), he returned to Gilfach Goch, and became reacquainted with my grandfather. It is impossible to know the nature of their business relationship. Was Bravo an employee or in some degree a partner? Nothing in the papers I salvaged answers the question.

It is just possible that, on their return to Gilfach, the Bravos were given accommodation at my grandfather's business address, 165 High Street. That kind of charity would be entirely consistent with what I have learned of Sam and Margaret Adams – and part of the arrangement may well have been that Harris Bravo looked after the shop. That is speculation. All I know now is that, on an occasion when my grandfather was out of the way, Bravo stole from him and disappeared. What he stole, again I can only guess. Most obviously cash and possibly other items of value that were portable. This may have meant that Dats was burdened with debts for the stolen stock such as jewellery and fancy goods from suppliers in London and elsewhere. I don't know whether Bravo was pursued. If he was, the pursuit was unsuccessful. Thinking about it now, I wonder why my mother and father said so little about an episode that, from the fragments of evidence I have been able to gather, probably occurred not long before I was born and my grandfather died.

Whether Bravo's abandoned wife and daughter remained in south Wales for weeks or months I cannot say, but eventually they went – I had always assumed to be reunited with the husband and father in London. But it now appears that, when he disappeared from Gilfach Goch, Harris Bravo did not go to London: he returned to Gilfach Bargoed. At least, that was where he died, alone, as the death certificate indicates, on 25 August 1944, aged seventy-six. His wife and children did return to London, where some scanty records of them can be found. Milly died, aged seventy-six, in Hackney, in the autumn of 1950. I still wonder whether, preserved in an ageing Home Counties memory, the faint recollection lingers of a story passed down by parents or grandparents, if not of theft and guilt, then at least of the generosity of a couple from a mining village in south Wales who took in a destitute wife and child when the husband fled.

I have also pondered the whereabouts of my grandfather when the theft occurred. He was, perhaps, in Italy. When I went up to Aberystwyth in 1952 my belongings travelled separately by train in a trunk, which for as long as I could remember had been stowed under my iron-framed single bed. Inside the cover of the trunk was the name 'Sam Adams' and our address, inscribed by Dats, who bought it for his visit to Italy. So far as I know, he travelled alone.

Descriptions of Italy in the 1920s that are concerned with the people rather than the remains of classical Rome, reveal an impoverished largely peasant culture. Poverty drove many to emigrate in search of a better life. Some came to the valleys of south Wales, where families founded Italian corner shop dynasties. There were at least three in Gilfach Goch – the Bacchettas, the Rabaiottis and the Tambinis. My grandfather was friendly with all of them and particularly close to the Tambinis. All three families were concerned to support the relatives they left behind, but sending money abroad was not easy. I was told that among the contents of the trunk when it went to Italy were bundles of clothing sent back home by Gilfach's expatriate Italians, and that the buttons of the clothes were cloth covered sovereigns and half-sovereigns. I do not know where Dats travelled in Italy, or what sights he saw. All that remains of the adventure is the gold smuggling story.

The connections my grandfather made with businesses in Cardiff persisted in attenuated form twenty years after his death. From time to time in those early days of 'hire purchase' we would receive letters from one or other of the long-established furniture stores asking about the credit-worthiness of Gilfach people. My father and Barbara would supply what information they could. George Murphy, the Punch-faced postman, who was familiar with domestic arrangements in most of the houses in the valley, was occasionally co-opted as adviser. The payment for this service was a shilling or two in little blocks of postage stamps.

***

My grandfather's business interests were not confined to furniture, fancy goods and electrical fitting. He was also a property owner, a would-be valleys rentier, though his concern for others was never likely to advance an ambition of that kind. On 15 March 1920, 8 Bryn Seion Terrace, Gilfach Goch, was 'assigned' to him, and on 8 April the same year a house at 107 High Street. The solicitor acting in these transactions was David Llewellyn, the lawyer son of William Llewellyn, the wealthy grocer of Ogmore Vale, and the address for correspondence with Samuel Adams was yet another house, 169 High Street, the address from which my father married. It is clear from other papers that he gave 107 High Street to his daughter Julia and her husband, Will Trethowan. Their daughter, Jean, told me he gave 8 Bryn Seion Terrace to the Salvation Army as a home for the brigade captain.

In 1922, Dats acquired properties in Coedely, a village just south of Tonyrefail, about four miles from Gilfach, and site of one of the biggest collieries in the area. This appears to have been as the result of a venture in which several investors shared: 'Coed-Ely Building Club No.1'. On 27 July 1922, at 'the final winding up of accounts', he paid £245 3s 0d and the house at 7 Collwyn Street was allotted to him. By this time he already owned three other houses in the village – 15, 17 and 19 Garth Street, which were subsequently leased to Margaret Adams, his wife, presumably for tax purposes, since there seems no other reason to have done so.

The Coedely properties generated a stack of papers, because from 1932 (or perhaps earlier; I can only refer to documents that survived) they were managed by J. Downes, an estate agent with an office in Tonyrefail. He collected rents, found new tenants when a house was vacated, kept an eye on properties and notified owners about maintenance needs. He charged ten per cent commission on the rents he collected. Statements from 5 September 1932 to 29 August 1938 show my grandparents received rental income of about £25 per quarter, from time to time reduced to £21 or £22 by the estate agent's expenses. The annual income would have been about £85, and it would have taken rather more than five years to recoup the initial investment.

One sheaf of papers gives details of the outlay on property maintenance. Materials and labour were usually supplied by Hammond & Co., a well-known ironmongers and building materials supplier, whose premises opposite the Boar's Head on Tonyrefail Square I remember well. The surviving invoices date from February 1932 to January 1940 and are for piffling amounts by 2015 standards. In March 1935, the cost of a special oven and grate bottom, firebricks, mortar, skirting, a pane of glass, four pounds of linseed oil putty, various screws, and haulage, was £2 1s 11d. The labour cost for repairing the back of the grate and fixing a new oven in the kitchen, repairing the front room grate, fixing new skirting, fixing a window sash and repairing a window was twelve shillings: total £2 13s 11d.

The invoices tell a story of broken sash windows (a recurring problem), damaged doors and door frames, the replacement of lavatory seats and pans and piping of various kinds, brickwork occasionally and, once, roof repairs, all notified by Downes and, in due course, put right by Hammond's men. There were delays in effecting repairs. On 5 June 1933 Downes wrote at the foot of his quarterly statement:

'All the houses on the left side of Garth St. caught the full force of the snow storm in March & shoots [*sic*] and chimneys were damaged, some chimneys down altogether.'

On 1 March 1937 he jotted a warning:

'The Sanitary Inspector is busy in this district ...' [and on 1 June] 'Those repairs were absolutely necessary. The wall and door almost down. I was terrified fearing a stone would fall on the children & then there would be a terrible fuss. Kind Regards.'

The houses seem to have been particularly prone to damage. Perhaps they were badly built, perhaps badly knocked about by tenants. As well as income, property ownership brought responsibility and expense.

***

Although my presence was not planned or anticipated at either, I attended the funerals of both Mam and Dats. Ten days old when my grandfather died suddenly on 6 December 1934, I was christened over his coffin. And I was four when Mam died 22 March 1939. Of course, I have no direct recall of either event. The stories I tell are part of an inheritance of memories bequeathed by my mother and my sisters.

Babs and Joan were already twelve and thirteen respectively when Dats died and remembered the day clearly. About four in the afternoon, he had come home from the day shift and in all likelihood had eaten a cooked dinner, which had been covered with a dish and kept warm on top of the oven. This was my father's routine as I well know, and I see them, father and son, together and still in working clothes, eating a meal prepared about midday for the rest of the family. Then my father would have hurried to wash away the pit dirt before joining my mother and the new baby in another room, perhaps the small sitting room we knew as the back room. She would be settled in her favourite padded basket chair, which was like a large nest that creaked and rustled comfortingly, drawn close to the fire in the red-tiled grate. It was the first week of December. Mam, having seen to the needs of husband and son, would also be there, leaving Dats in the kitchen with Joan, Barbara and their twenty-year-old cousin Bloom, who, when his parents moved to Port Talbot, had remained with his grandparents to attend the county school in Bridgend, and afterwards because he had a job in the Squint colliery office.

The three grandchildren would have been seated at the table in the kitchen, and Dats in the wooden armchair beside the fireplace, his feet on the steel fender. The top of the oven, close on his left, where earlier the covered dinner plates had rested, would have been piled with sticks drying for the morrow's fire, while before the glowing coals the brass stand gleamed with reflections. The iron kettle would be humming to itself on the further hob, a shining pillar of black-leaded bricks. It would be a big fire, burning lustily.

For tea Bloom and my sisters were having currant buns. Bloom had the gift of making others laugh – on that occasion by dissecting and scrutinising a bun, which seemed to have very few currants. He extracted those he could find, cut them into smaller portions and made a 'currant sandwich' with a slice of bread and butter. Joan remembered all this not for the silliness of it, or because Dats laughed so much tears ran down his cheeks, but because, soon after, he went upstairs for a nap, as he always did, and an hour later, when Mam took him the usual cup of tea, he was dead.

I was told what family and neighbours said at the time. It was as though he had made a space in the world for me – 'For the Lord giveth and the Lord taketh away' and 'One goes that another may come'. All who knew and remembered my grandfather said he was 'a lovely man', benign and philanthropic, though with far lesser means and influence, not unlike that Thomas Adams who had been Lord Mayor of London. My cousin Jean told me that during the 1926 strike he paid the food bills of impoverished miners' families at Pegler's. At this time, too, Mam was one of the team at the Bryn Seion Chapel soup kitchen, as old photographs show, helping to feed the unemployed and their families.

The funeral service was conducted by the Vicar of St Barnabas, although Mam and Dats were staunch Salvationists. I recall a story of Dats being converted at a 'knee-drill', and they regularly stood with the Salvation Army's silver band and sang in the street. My grandmother was reputed to have a fine, clear voice that could carry across the valley. Surely the Army, too, was represented at the funeral, but all I know from repeated telling is that I was christened over the coffin and when the vicar asked what name I should be given, it was Mam who answered 'Samuel'. My mother added 'John', perhaps because it was her, still-living, father's name, so that I should bear a vestigial signature of both grandfathers. But long afterwards she would say she had been weak and confused by birth and death following so closely and had simply said the first name that came into her head.

She did not like old-fashioned Samuel, or Sam, and never once addressed me by either. At home I was John. It was not the most convenient choice. I already had not one, but two first cousins, both only a little older, who had been given the same name. For years afterwards, to avoid confusion with John Love, the son of Uncle Gordon and Aunty Olga, my mother's family called me Sonny.

If my mother is to be believed, while awaiting my arrival she had cherished quite other plans for my naming: I was to be Mark, she said, or Marcus. I am sure I could have become reconciled to either, but I was plain John, and so I remained. Outside the house and family, at school, among friends, as I grew older I was increasingly Sam. It was as though I had a nickname (as some who used it believed), but it was my own first name and I grew into it. It remained unfashionable and for much of my life, unusual, though that has changed in recent years. For me, it holds a sense of connection with the past, and with a man I heartily wish had lived longer so that I could have known him a little.

Of Mam, my father's mother, I have memories, but nothing really of her appearance or her manner beyond what old photographs can supply. I cherish the notion that we spoke Welsh together, but suspect it is insecurely founded, for my father had no Welsh, or if he did, kept it very much to himself. In the memory I have of her, I am three or perhaps just four, and she is holding my hand as I walk up the road with her.

At Spearing's, the small delicatessen, she stops to gossip with old Mrs Spearing, who is standing in the doorway. Like any irritating child I tug at her hand to draw her away. Then she is ill, confined to the big front bedroom with the polished heavy, dark furniture. I cannot remember being at her bedside, but one day when I am doing I know not what, there is a commotion above and running feet along the landing, and I rush to the stairs and start to climb, peering upwards to see. But I am quickly caught and carried down. And that is all.

Funerals were attended by men only; the women of the household were expected to prepare sandwiches, cakes and tea for the mourners when they returned from the graveside. It seems likely there was a funeral service for Mam at the church or the Salvation Army temple, a simple single-storey building at the foot of a steep mountain of slag. I wanted to go to the funeral, but was told children didn't go and, besides, I didn't have a bowler hat. Left to my own devices, I went next door to old Mr Lester, who always wore a bowler, and asked could I borrow it to go to the funeral. He might have thought this was some kind of game and, seeing no harm in the gesture anyway, handed me his hat. I waited in the front garden until I saw the cortege approaching, then ran out through the gate with my bowler, stood at the kerb and held out my arm. One of the big black cars stopped and I was taken on board. I do not remember any of this, but was told about it often enough.

Sam and Margaret Adams were both born in 1869. As I look back over the record of births of Williamses and Adamses in successive generations inscribed in the Family Bible and enumerated in censuses since 1841, even allowing for what now seem terrible mortality rates, I am astounded and moved by realisation of the great number of aunts, uncles and cousins at various removes somewhere out there. Our family tree, if one could ever be completed, would not be a shapely specimen, but dense and impenetrable as an African thorn. The account given in these pages is of but the slenderest branch, little more than a twig, of that shapeless, teeming bush.

Nine

I AM NOT sure now where I heard how my father was spared the horrors of the Western Front. I am certain he didn't tell me. Nor did he talk about the turbulence and suffering that afflicted scores of pit villages like ours in the twenty-five years between 1914 and 1939, and the politics of the coalfield. It was never discussed in the house by my mother, whose conversation was very wide-ranging, nor was it mentioned by aunts and uncles who had lived through those years. Perhaps my family differed in this respect from others, but if within their families my friends had heard of strikes, lock-outs, hunger marches, they did not speak of them to me. No reference was made in school to industrial strife and prolonged economic depression. Apart from a few isolated, decontextualised anecdotes, one from my mother, another about the Samaritan acts of Mam and Dats, my knowledge of events has been gathered in later life from history books, and given an emotional charge by the poetry of Idris Davies.

My father, born in June 1896, was just eighteen at the beginning of the war in July 1914. Like many thousands of young men he was eager to volunteer for the army, but was saved by the intervention of *his* father, whether through rational argument at home or dramatically at the recruitment office I cannot say. Army regulations of the time would not have allowed him to serve overseas until he was nineteen, and when conscription began, he would have been deemed exempt on the grounds it was 'expedient in the national interests' that he remained in the pit. The exemption clause in the Military Services Act of January 1916 recognised the damaging fall in coal production that resulted from the exodus of miners to the ranks (40,000 from south Wales alone) in the early stages of the war.

In 1913, virtually on the eve of the war, almost a fifth of total British coal production came from south Wales. The output of the Rhondda valleys had almost doubled to approximately ten million tons over the preceding quarter of a century. This scale of increase, which was echoed in other Welsh mining areas including the anthracite valleys in the south-west of the coalfield, was achieved against a background of economic uncertainty, not readily observable in the short term, created by the early commitment of a high proportion of Welsh coal production to export markets overseas. Mine owners' relentless pressure to force down the costs of production, principally the wages of miners, in order to maintain a competitive price in the marketplace, was a recipe for strife, while widespread geological problems, low investment and the slow pace of modernisation in the industry contributed to the underlying precariousness of the situation. The Cambrian Combine strike that began in the Rhondda and Gilfach Goch in November 1910 and ended in October 1911 with a return to work on the owners' terms, with its violence on both sides and legacy of bitterness, was only one in a long line of disputes, which continued despite the outbreak of war. A patriotic agreement in 1915 between the trade unions and Lloyd George, then Minister of Munitions, did not deter the South Wales Miners' Federation from declaring an official strike for a higher standard wage rate in the same year. After ten days the miners won and, under the leadership of men like Noah Ablett, Arthur Cook and Arthur Horner, with the example of the Russian Revolution before them, they became increasingly militant. This was when Maerdy at the top of the Rhondda Fach gained its reputation as 'Little Moscow'.

The profits of coal owners increased hugely from the beginning of the war, while they continued to resist their employees' wage demands in the face of increases in the cost of living. When, in November 1916, the powers of the

Defence of the Realm Act (August 1914), which had earlier given the government control of the railways, shipping and munitions, were extended to include coal mining in south Wales, it must have seemed to the workers that this quasi-nationalisation, albeit under the imperative of war, placed within reach the goal of securing 'the full fruits of their industry and the most equitable distribution thereof that may be possible upon the basis of common ownership of the means of production, distribution, and exchange' (to quote Clause IV of the British Labour Party Constitution, 1918). A miners' ballot overwhelmingly in support of strike action prompted Lloyd George's government early in March 1919 to set up a commission chaired by Sir John Sankey to look into wages, hours and nationalisation in the coal industry. With faith in the justice of their cause and trust in the fair dealing of politicians, the miners decided to work on and await the outcome. Within the month the commission reported in favour of increasing wages and cutting working hours, and in June a second report showed a majority of members favoured nationalisation. In August, the government, adopting a characteristic political stratagem, gave its response: it would establish a new Department of Mines and set up regional joint committees of owners and men, and a fund to improve social conditions in mining areas. Of increased wages, shorter hours, nationalisation, it said nothing.

In October 1920 the south Wales miners finally persuaded those in other parts of Britain to join them in a strike for higher wages. In a fortnight Lloyd George's government conceded and granted an increase of two shillings a shift. Men were able to earn as much as £5 a week, but the relative prosperity didn't last. This was the period when radical socialism in the south Wales coalfield grew into a mass movement, marching with hope and expectation towards a promised land and, in the words of the great Marxist historian Gwyn Alf Williams, 'marched instead into a blizzard which killed their Wales stone dead'.

The coal industries of France, Belgium and Poland were reviving, America was opening rich new coalfields, and Germany was offering coal gratis as war reparations to its former enemies. The price of British coal collapsed – in south Wales, which relied heavily on its export trade, by fifty per cent. The government washed its hands of the business and on 31 March 1921 returned the pits to the owners, who immediately halved wages. There were lulls in the storm, when, briefly, economic conditions abroad once more favoured British coal: a record 78 million tons were exported in 1923, and unemployment among miners in Wales as late as April 1924 stood at less than two per cent. A year later British exports were hard hit by the upward revaluation of the pound following Chancellor Winston Churchill's decision to return to the gold standard, exacerbating already unfavourable economic conditions. By August 1925, unemployment had risen to more than twenty-eight per cent: the beginning of the Depression. Not long before, coalfield employers had torn up the 1924 wage scales and the seven-hour working day agreement that had been a victory for the miners in 1919. The miners' response was predictable, and on this occasion railway workers and seamen were prepared to support them. Baldwin's government delayed what threatened to be a crippling three-pronged action by setting up another commission, chaired by Sir Herbert Samuel, thus affording it nine months' breathing space during which it planned how it would deal with a general strike. The ultimate answer would be to invoke the Emergency Powers Act (1920), which would give it the right to declare a state of emergency and, among other measures, call in the military.

The commission turned down nationalisation as a solution and recommended a reduction in miners' wages – in respect of which the government gave the owners a free hand. They proposed a wage cut of thirteen per cent and a one-hour extension of the working day. When these terms were rejected, on 30 April 1926 the employers responded with a lock-out.

The miners had the support of the Trades Union Congress and when the government withdrew from discussions on 2 May a general strike was called which lasted ten days. On 12 May the TUC, persuaded that proposals put forward by Samuel, the chair of the commission, were worthy of consideration, called off the strike, leaving the miners to fight on alone.

> Do you remember 1926? The slogans and the penny concerts,
> The jazz-bands and the moorland picnics,
> And the slanderous tongues of famous cities?
> Do you remember 1926? The great dream and the swift disaster,
> The fanatic and the traitor, and more than all,
> The bravery of the simple, faithful folk?

Thus Idris Davies in 'Gwalia Deserta'. He had become a miner's helper in Abertysswg Colliery as a fourteen year old in 1919 and lost the little finger of his left hand when a large stone, narrowly missing his head, fell on it a few months before the strike in 1926. He knew what it was to labour at the coalface, and it is clear where his sympathies lie. 'Slogans'? Yes, like that of miners' leader Arthur Cook: 'Not a minute on the day, not a penny off the pay.' The 'slanderous tongues'? Those of the press barons and their newspapers, including the *Western Mail*, which vilified the miners. 'The great dream'? That of workers in all occupations united against oppression, and winning. In the autumn, strikers in the English coalfields began drifting back to the pits, but it was not until 19 November that utter destitution forced those in south Wales to capitulate. Even then, not all returned to work: there were no jobs for some 24,000 (including all those identified as politically active) who had begun the strike in May. The employers introduced regional wage scales and the men found themselves back in unmodernised, inefficient pits, where accident and fatality rates were high, on ten shillings for an eight-hour day – effectively about fifty per cent of the pay for the seven-hour days they had worked in 1921.

Groups of miners singing for pennies on London street corners became a common sight during the strike and for a considerable time afterwards as successive governments failed to tackle unemployment. The Wall Street Crash of October 1929, which badly affected export industries, made matters worse. In 1929 unemployment in Wales stood at nineteen per cent; in 1931 it reached thirty-five per cent, and in August 1932 almost forty-three per cent. In 1938, sixty-two per cent of the unemployed in the twin valleys of the Rhondda had been out of work for three years or more. It is not surprising that, during the 1930s, 50,000 people dragged up their Rhondda roots and left.

In the year I was born, 1934, the coalition National government under Ramsay MacDonald recognised that unemployment remained a desperately serious problem outside the English midlands and south-east, but proved incapable of doing anything constructive about it. In November 1936, when I was just two, Edward VIII, on a visit to Blaenavon, famously said, 'Something must be done', though nothing was. John Davies, whose excellent *A History of Wales* provides most of the detail in the foregoing greatly abbreviated account, shows that even within a month of the Second World War there were few signs of economic recovery in south Wales. And as a boy, even as a young adult, I knew nothing of all this. I am fairly sure my immediate family did not suffer in the way my wife's family and most others suffered, for long, impoverished, grinding years, because Sam Adams, my entrepreneurial grandfather and colliery overman, had assiduously built a barrier between the economic adversities of the coalfield and those he loved.

Ten

MY FATHER WAS responsible for everything electrical in the Squint. He worked the day shift but was on call at any hour. On odd occasions throughout my childhood the entire household would be roused in the middle of the night by loud knocking on the front door. My father would rise and soon after I would hear him hurrying down the path, and would turn again to sleep while he entered a world of dangers beyond my imagining. Failure of the pumps that prevented the mine from flooding, a typical emergency, would mean that he would be working in water up to his waist while repairing the equipment.

In 1946, shortly before nationalisation of the coal industry, he suffered the accident that changed his life. He was underground on that occasion, repairing a coal cutter, a huge machine with an action rather like a chainsaw, set up to cut deep horizontal slots along a seam, allowing the miners to use their picks to strike down the coal, which could then be shovelled into drams and brought to the surface. The coal cutter my father was working on was powered by an electrical current of more than 700 volts, which was controlled by a remote switch about twenty-five yards off. He was holding the cable that fed the current to the machine with his bare right hand when the switch was turned on. The surge of electricity would not allow him to release his grip and, for the seconds it took for someone to run to the switch and turn it off, the current coursed through his body. Colliers present at the scene spoke later of the shower of sparks that enveloped him and the stench of burning flesh as the wire ate into his hand. It was remarkable he survived.

Not much could be done for his hand. It was roughly dressed and his arm put in a sling. He walked to the surface, then along the steep rubble path past the colliery office, over the railway lines at the station and up High Street to the house, where he waited for the ambulance. Nothing would have prevented him coming home to show Mama he was all right. He was taken to the infirmary in Cardiff and more than three months passed before she saw him again.

After charred flesh had been trimmed and the wound tidied, doctors were able to see that the burn had taken the tops of fingers and destroyed the nerves and sinews in the palm that give our hands flexibility, strength and sensitivity. They decided an attempt should be made to save what remained and he was sent to the burns unit at Chepstow, where during and after the war early miracles of plastic surgery had been performed on badly burned airmen. There a lump of flesh was cut from his abdomen and sewn into the damaged hand, and then the hand sewn to the hole in the abdomen so that the graft would take, as eventually it did. Weeks later, when the hand was removed from its nest of flesh, a layer of skin was shaved from his thigh to cover the deep wound that remained there. He once showed me the big, discoloured scar below his ribs on the left side, but he never spoke of the operations, or what it was like to spend days, and nights, with one hand attached to his body. There was very little communication with him throughout this time. Chepstow was a long way off.

I think he was probably in hospital during the long, terrible winter of 1947. The snow began in January and persisted until March. I remember walking over drifts between the hedges at the crossroads entrance to the valley that were so deep I could have reached up and touched the telegraph wires. Other than hazardously on foot, it was not possible to get into or out of the valley. Shops opened but could not be restocked. Bakers ran out of flour. Eventually news came that milk and bread had been brought from Tonyrefail, but only as far as the top of Ton hill, beyond the deepest drifts. Gilfach was again as remote a spot as it had been a century before. I hated the snow then and have done ever since. Electricity was cut off for weeks. We withdrew to our back kitchen, where the fire was well tended, and in the evenings played cards by candlelight.

My father had large, square hands, the hands of a man who, from his youth, had known hard and heavy work. His time as baker's assistant was never mentioned and was surely the briefest of interludes before the colliery and absorption in electrical wiring and equipment took over until it became second nature to him. His thick fingers were deft and delicate with the intricacies of machines. He was inventive, too; if the parts were not available to finish a job or effect a repair, he would create them. He was intensely practical and resourceful, a manual pragmatist. As a young man he was responsible for the installation and maintenance of machines and equipment at the Squint colliery, and played a part in the electrification of Gilfach. So far as I was aware his hair, though dense, as it remained, was always silver, and he came home in his pit dirt, sat at the end of the table in the kitchen and ate his dinner, kept warm on top of the oven, with black tea sweetened with a little sugar. He did not talk about his day, how dirty and often disgusting it was underground, the quotidian dangers and sheer slog of it. From time to time there were jobs to be done about the house, like chopping sticks for the fire, but soon he would bath and come downstairs with shining face and hair, put his feet up, begin to read *The Echo*, and fall asleep.

He and I came to an understanding when I was very young. Probably my earliest memory is of climbing the stairs on hands and knees, so that the pattern on the carpet and the gleaming brass stair rods are very close. I am moving slowly, under protest, and he gives me a tap on the backside. I turn and smack his hand, and he smacks me. I cannot recall a dispute arising between us in all the years that followed and I never defied him again. It was not his fault and, I suppose, not mine that we had no common interest, though love bound us absolutely. I was, and am, inept with machinery, while it fascinated him. But then, I don't believe he ever read a book, unless it was the handbook of some new piece of equipment.

Until his accident he always had a motorbike. The one I recall was the Harley Davidson, an enormous machine painted olive drab, the colour required by the US War Department when the manufacturer was commissioned to supply bikes for American forces in the First World War. The sidecar was olive drab too and proportionally large, like a blunt-prowed boat. There was room for an adult and child in the chassis and, with the dickey open, it could accommodate two more children on a bench seat. One of my earliest memories is of travelling in the sidecar to St Nicholas, in the Vale of Glamorgan, to visit kindly, silver-haired 'Uncle Tim', then headmaster of the local primary school. This must have taken place shortly before the war. In September 1939 petrol was rationed and not long after none was available at all for private motorists.

He maintained the bike himself, taking it apart expertly and putting it together again. Sometimes, at weekends, he would go up the path cut out of grey colliery shale to the black shed, for which he paid ground rent to the Lanelay Estate, owners of most of the land and the mineral rights in our part of Gilfach. I liked going with him on these occasions, though not to watch and learn what he was doing. I played with discarded pieces of older bikes, or watched housemartins that had plastered a nest to one of the rafters and, feeding their brood, flew unerringly in and out through small holes rusted in the corrugated sheets. By the time petrol rationing ended in 1950, my father was no longer able to grip anything with his right hand and controlling a motorbike was out of the question. The Harley Davidson was sold for a paltry sum and the one true source of pleasure outside home and family went out of my father's life.

I recall my mother saying, with a hint of pride, that he vaulted five-bar gates with ease, presumably in their courting days, and he mentioned how he competed at work with other young men in punching six-inch nails into the wooden doors of the engine house, though I have wondered how they managed that. So he was strong as a young man and agile enough, but I do not know that he ever played football, rugby or any games. He would have had very little time for them, since when he wasn't in the colliery he was working for his father's business. Given the time his labour earned for me, I played games, with much enthusiasm if indifferent skill. He didn't watch when I played at the Welfare Park or discuss rugby with me, but he was happy to see how keen I was, and applied on my behalf for Cardiff RFC season tickets, which brought me wonderful club rugby and the chance to go to international matches. He followed boxing in the newspapers and on the wireless, as most did then, while the fight between Tommy Farr of Tonypandy and Joe Louis was fresh in the memory. Jimmy Wilde, the Tylorstown Terror, still lived over the mountain, and Freddie Welsh of Pontypridd and Jim Driscoll of Cardiff, two other great champions, were not long dead, but the only sporting ambition he had was to ride his motorbike in the races that used to be held at public parks here and there in the south Wales valleys.

His technical skills advanced in step with developments in the equipment and machinery he handled daily, but his tastes were unsophisticated, moulded by the experiences and mores of the society in which he grew to adulthood. On the wireless, he enjoyed listening to brass bands, but hated jazz trumpet, and couldn't stand the voice of Cilla Black. He usually fell asleep promptly in front of the television, but the merest glimpse of her at the height of her popularity would propel him out of his comfortable chair to attend to some chore. He was equally intolerant of male ballet dancers. 'Like a lot of prancing entires,' he would mutter as he left, with the emphasis in the first syllable of 'entires', a critique understandable only to those familiar with horses.

He took pleasure in my sister Joan's passion for horses and riding. I was not surprised by his confidence with horses: that was no different from everything he did. But I should have been. Where did he gain the knowledge and the calm competence with which he handled these large animals that

147

invariably made me nervous? I believe I now know the answer. When he was young, horse-drawn vehicles were the norm on Gilfach's streets. More significantly, three of his uncles, his father's brothers, were employed as hauliers, and as an electrician underground he worked alongside horses daily in confined spaces. Although I had not been aware of it, horses had been part of his life since childhood. He knew better than to beat or bully them; he commanded in a voice of authority and they generally obeyed. I remember watching him hold Rhona's still unbroken foal by the halter and when despite his calming tones it persisted in bucking and rearing up, to my amazement he smacked it on the nose. The foal stood still, long legs splayed, blinking, and then allowed itself to be led away, docile. Although he didn't ride, he sometimes wore breeches and enjoyed rare visits to horse shows and gymkhanas.

He was above all a worker. He would never have thought it, far less expressed the notion, but what sustained him was the dignity of work, indissolubly connected with love of family. He rose early, often before five o'clock, to clear the ashes of the previous day's fires. Transferred in my teens to the bedroom above the kitchen, I would hear the clatter of the bucket, the raking of dead coals, the shovel grinding on the stone bottom of the grate, accompanied by terrible coughing over the first cigarette of the day, and in a few minutes the roar of the new fire in the chimney-breast behind my head. Once the soot-blackened kettle had boiled he would make a cup of tea for my mother and then sit to his solitary breakfast before putting on his pit boots and cap and setting out. Other than when he was in hospital, I don't think he missed a day. He abhorred laziness. 'Idle bugger', was his most withering term of opprobrium, delivered *sotto voce* on an occasion I well remember, as he exchanged nods with a local Labour councillor who lived across the road from us a few doors down from the Vaughans.

In the final weeks of treatment at the burns unit, my father was allowed to walk outside and into Chepstow. There he bought a copy of the sheet music of 'Coming Home', a popular song of the years immediately after the war, and put it in the post:

Coming home my darling,
Coming home to you,
I can see your bright eyes shining,
In the cloud there's a silver lining.

The oak table in the front room was extended and we had a party to welcome him. It was 1947; food was still rationed and we had little enough to offer. The three ducks that Joan had brought home as ducklings from Cardiff Market were sacrificed. They were well grown but had become pets and, roasted on a platter, we believed we could still identify them individually. After his long journey, my father had as little appetite as we, but relatives and friends enjoyed the treat.

Joan told me that, by the time he came out of hospital, post-nationalisation, four or more men were employed in the Squint to do the job he had done alone – though he did have the help of Dick John, who carried the enormous bag of tools, a portable workshop, which he needed to meet all the problems that might arise anywhere in the pit. Once, when I was very young, I met this amiable assistant, whose name was puzzling: to me he was John Dick. For loss of the use of his right hand Dada was offered lump sum compensation of a few hundred pounds. If he had taken it I think that could have ended his working life. He opted instead to receive a weekly sum of rather less than £2.

I have no memory of a hiatus between his return from hospital and beginning to work again, but there must surely have been one. In a brief letter from the chief accountant's office of the NCB in Porth, he was told that he would be paid arrears amounting to £297 15s 11d 'due from 7/7/47 to 24/11/51, resulting from the revision of your pre-accident average to that of head electrician'. I am unsure whether this refers to his rate of pay as a worker or his compensation. In either case it recognises that at the time of the accident he was chief electrician at the Squint, and it suggests that he returned to the payroll in July 1947. Other than that I have a very hazy notion of the chronology of these events. The concern for the welfare of workers that helped inspire the movement towards nationalisation of heavy industries surely saved him from the scrapheap. Where exactly, and in what capacity, he began working again is another blank. Nor is it easy to guess: after all, while he was knowledgeable about electrical equipment, for any tasks requiring fine manipulation of tools and machinery he was severely handicapped.

When the Squint closed in 1949 he was deployed to assist scrap dealers contracted to clear the site. No one knew better where the more valuable metals were to be found, because they were virtually all connected with electrical equipment. Once or twice a scrap dealer came to the house with my father for his usual mid-morning tea break. One showed me the fat rolls of £1 and £5 notes that bulged his pocket. A great deal of money was made out of pit closures, though not by the men who had given their working lives, and their health, to mining.

Where he went next I have no idea, except that he continued to work for the NCB. A single surviving pay docket shows that in December 1952 he was employed in the electricians' workshop at Park Colliery, near Treorci in the Rhondda Fawr, about fifteen miles from Gilfach, where by that time all the pits had closed. He was bussed there daily with other displaced Gilfach mineworkers: his pay, £10 17s 2d after stoppages, included a 5s 2d travelling allowance. He was one of a workforce of more than 2,000, and when Park merged with the neighbouring Dare Colliery in 1955 it became the biggest pit in south Wales. The upper Rhondda Fawr was a far-left Labour stronghold and my father enjoyed the political banter of the workshop. In deference to my mother who was, of course, influenced by her father, he considered himself

Tory (though I am sure he was fundamentally apolitical). His fellow electricians were delighted to have someone whose views differed from theirs to enliven debate and when he left Park they clubbed together to buy him a watch, of which he was justifiably proud. It was the only tangible recognition of what he had given to the coal industry, and that was more than most received.

My father's last years in mining were spent at Cwm Colliery, Beddau, near Pontypridd, another large and productive pit. When it closed in 1986, coal reserves estimated at nine million tons were abandoned. About the time he arrived it was being linked underground with the colliery in Coedely, the village where, long before, his father had bought houses to let to collier tenants. At Cwm he worked on the repair and maintenance of fifteen-ton diesel locomotives that hauled coal along thirteen miles of underground roadways. A photograph of him from this period shows a diminutive figure turned away from the camera inspecting a huge, gleaming machine. He retired 17 June 1961, his birthday, aged 65. He had seen the coal industry develop from the early days of electrification to modern mechanisation, and then many of the pits closed, the sites gradually cleared, the tips landscaped. He lived to see Gilfach Goch, a convenient test bed for land reclamation schemes because it is a small, separate valley, well on its way to being completely transformed from the place where he had grown up, and losing its sense of purpose.

***

John Love, my mother's father, known to us as Dada Love, was born in 1868 in the parish of Wellow, north-east Somerset, not far from Radstock, or indeed from Bath. He was the first son and fourth of ten children of Jeremiah and Rebecca Love, and a near coeval of Samuel, my Adams grandfather. Wellow had long been a coal mining area and, about the time of John's birth, his father was a coal weigher – a position of some significance and trust, since miners' wages were calculated on the weight of coal they cut and loaded. At the 1881 Census, Jeremiah's occupation is given as 'coal miner', but a decade later he was a colliery overman, a promoted position with managerial and safety responsibilities underground, the role my father's father also eventually held. It is no surprise that his four sons followed him down the pit. At thirteen, John was already a miner, as was Sam Adams in Gilfach Goch. By 1891 he had left home, but not mining. He was in lodgings in Bedwellty, near Blackwood, Monmouthshire, with a couple named Edwards and their three young children, who were from Radstock, and whom he might possibly have known before crossing the Bristol Channel. George Edwards, too, was a miner.

My mother told me that her father had come to south Wales because he had been recommended as an able musician who could bring lustre and leadership to the colliery brass band. Perhaps George Edwards was responsible for the recommendation. John Love certainly possessed a good deal of musical ability. Later, in the Rhondda, he was prominent as a conductor of oratorios, and (as we have seen) when the Workmen's Hall, Gilfach Goch, was formally opened in July 1924, at each performance throughout the week of celebrations there was a 'Grand Orchestra – Conductor J. Love Esq.'. He was familiar with several instruments and an accomplished violinist, and he took pains to pass his musical knowledge on to his children. How long he lived as a lodger in Bedwellty is beyond guessing. It was long enough, anyway, for him to make the acquaintance of a young woman who lived nearby named Mary Jane Stokes. Later, in 1891, they married.

My mother also brought us a story of a rather grand family connection. This one says that we are related to Bishop Lewis of Llandaff. Richard Lewis was born in 1821, the second son of a considerable Pembrokeshire landowner. He was educated at Oxford and, his older brother being principal heir to their father's property, committed himself to the Church. After experience as a curate in England, he was appointed Vicar of Amroth in 1847. He applied to the Bishop of St Davids, Dr Connop Thirwell, for institution to the Rectory of Lampeter Velfrey, close to his family home, Llanddewi Velfrey, and may have been surprised when Thirwell, an Englishman who had learned Welsh, insisted he must first pass an examination in the language. Lewis had from boyhood spoken Welsh 'with servants and labourers', but because he was found unable to converse 'upon any grave topic', he failed the test. After much legal and ecclesiastical argument, ultimately involving the Archbishop of Canterbury, he was allowed a resit. This time he was declared competent in Welsh and became rector in 1852. He proved energetic and capable, with a talent for administration. Despite the controversy, no grudges were borne on either side and he rose steadily in the Church hierarchy. He became Bishop of Llandaff in 1883, continued to speak and preach in Welsh (though there were critics of its quality) and, in his turn, insisted that candidates for induction in parishes where Welsh was spoken should themselves speak the language. He died in 1905, lauded in *Yr Haul*, the Church journal, as '*Yr hen Esgob anwyl*'.

What has 'the dear old Bishop' to do with us? My maternal grandmother was the daughter of Samuel Stokes, who, though born in Bedwellty, was of parents who had earlier come from Somerset, and Catherine Lewis. It is from Catherine the story comes and, as I have become accustomed to finding, without supporting evidence. But I have a photograph that seems to me to lend credence to it. It brings together four generations – my mother and her first child, my sister Joan, with her mother, and her grandmother, Catherine. Grandma Stokes was then in her seventies and, judging by appearances, in excellent health and perfectly capable of passing her family history on to grown-up grandchildren. Why would she bother to tell them an untruth?

Catherine was born in Cwmavon, her father Thomas Lewis having come to the ironworks there from Llanarth,

Cardiganshire. This is warmer, for Llanarth is much nearer Bishop Lewis's Pembrokeshire home than any part of Monmouthshire. While accessible information about the bishop's immediate family shows he cannot be directly connected to the ironworker in Cwmavon, there is the possibility of a collateral link. David Lewis of Henllan, the bishop's grandfather, married Elizabeth daughter of another wealthy family. They had two sons and four daughters. John, the elder son, was heir to the estate – a pattern repeated in the next generation, as we have seen. What happened to Owen Evans Lewis, the younger son, and to *his* children, who would have been the bishop's cousins, remains a puzzle. I choose to think that, with little by way of an inheritance, this young man drifted north to Llanarth, where he married and fathered Thomas Lewis; and Thomas, in turn, followed a well-worn path from rural Cardiganshire to find work in the industrial south-west, around Aberavon, where he met and married another Elizabeth, by whom he had a daughter, Catherine, who became my great-grandmother. And she carefully preserved for her children, and her children's children, that wisp of a family connection of which she was proud, that she was second cousin to the bishop who sat on the throne of St Teilo in Llandaff Cathedral. She did not pass on her language. In the 1891 Census, whereas her husband, Samuel Stokes, spoke English, Catherine declared she spoke Welsh, and her first child, Mary Jane, my grandmother, both Welsh and English, though there was no hint of the former in the years I knew her.

I am sure my mother preserved her allegiance to the Anglican Church because of this notion of a relationship with Bishop Lewis. She never to my knowledge attended services, although she might have done when she was younger and able to walk normally. She always carried in her purse a large and rather fine silver crucifix, with a loop at the top, the sort a priest might wear, probably the gift of her mother. At her prompting I joined the church choir. This, after a bomb blast had rendered the parish church unusable, entailed a walk of about a mile down to the mission church in the City, and often, with Malcolm, a friend and fellow chorister, running the gauntlet of gangs of City kids, who recognised from our Sunday-best that we were outsiders. I remained faithful to church and choir and was for a time attracted by the language and drama of liturgy and the Bible. In my teens I occasionally read the lesson at the eagle lectern during services, and taught a Sunday school class. I believe my mother would have been pleased if I had discovered a vocation, but I did not, and when I went up to Aberystwyth, church attendance ceased, though not from loss of faith; I simply allowed myself to become an idle backslider.

The uncles, aunts and cousins I knew and remember well from my childhood and while growing up were almost all from my mother's family, the Loves, where there were ten children. I also have a clear recollection of her widowed mother, Mama Love, whom I saw quite frequently at the home in Glamorgan Terrace on the unmade road behind our house which she shared with her daughter, my Aunty Lil, and bald Uncle Percy, the undersized colliery blacksmith with a Woodbine habit and a terrible chest. She was a pretty woman, like an older version of my mother – small, silver-haired, always neatly dressed in dark clothes – and she preserved about her an air of lovely tranquillity. While others bustled at household chores, she remained calmly smiling. Goodness knows, she had worked hard as a young woman and deserved the peace of her later years. She was in her seventies when, with Lil and Percy, she moved to Barry where they lived with Auntie Winnie and Uncle Tom in the grocer's shop on the Parade, overlooking public gardens and the sea. It was there she died, aged eighty, in 1952, during my first term at Aberystwyth. I did not attend her funeral, but I think of her now with something like awe. This woman, my mother's mother, whom I knew well, was seven at the time of the Zulu War and as a girl and young woman was certainly aware of the Boer Wars – though she had more pressing concerns as wife and mother, bearing and nurturing a rapidly growing brood and supporting an ambitious husband during periods of great turbulence in the south Wales coalfield. She lived on through two world wars, saw the Valleys communities reach their peak of population and productivity and the beginning of their long decline into aimlessness. She embodied a history of modern times, had I but realised it.

I am certain Dada Love had a profound influence on my mother while she was growing up. She spoke of him with pride and admiration. He seems to have brought to south Wales a clear sense of his otherness as an Englishman and had no inclination to learn Welsh, even if the young woman he married had some grasp of the language. He wore a blue ribbon in his buttonhole, Mama told me, to show his commitment to the Tory cause. It would take a bold man to reveal political allegiance other than Labour anywhere in the Valleys at that time, and for decades to come. My sister Joan told me that on special occasions he would produce a half-sovereign for her from his waistcoat pocket, and that he took holidays alone on the Channel Islands – where, she said, he had a mistress. While I gawped, she sat smiling at my disbelief. Whatever the truth of that, it was from her father that my mother derived her musical skill. She played the piano well, was an excellent sight-reader and fine accompanist. All her brothers and sisters learned to play a musical instrument, with what varied levels of enthusiasm and competence I cannot say, but their father insisted they practise regularly, and together as a family band. When he died in the summer of 1940, in his seventy-fourth year, I was five. He must have sat me on his knee, held me by the hand, talked to me, and he seems to have been a memorable character, but not to me, alas: I have not the faintest recollection of him.

The Love family, like the Adamses, led a peripatetic life before settling in Gilfach Goch. When they were first married, John and Mary Jane lived at Blackwood, and it was there that their first child, Winifred, was born in 1892. Soon after, they moved to Newbridge, in the Ebbw Valley of Monmouthshire. There a further seven children were born: Lilian Alice in 1894, Catherine Rebecca (who was always known as Cissie) in 1896, my mother, Edith Maud, in 1898, Hubert Elsworth in 1900, Bernice Lindlie in 1901, Leslie Gilmore in 1902, and Annie Gwendoline in 1904. Gordon Hayward was born in New Park Terrace, Clydach Vale, in 1907, and that was also the birthplace in March 1909 of John Cyril, whom I knew as Uncle Cyril.

That my grandparents had this crowd of children was not, at the time, remarkable, but the choice of pretentious second names for several of them was. There is nothing in the family histories of the Lewises and Loves to account for Lindlie, Hayward, Elsworth and Gilmore. They were meant to confer distinction upon those who bore them, and perhaps they did. With the possible exception of Aunty Lil and my mother, they all stand out in my memory as vigorous, confident people, who smiled a lot, as though the world was on their side.

Uncle Les as a teenager, newly qualified from Smith's Nautical College in Cardiff as a wireless operator, was interviewed for his first job with a steamship line. 'Can you be a gentleman?' was the key, if not only, question. While others dithered, 'I'll do my best ...', Les answered boldly, 'Yes' and was immediately appointed. He was the star of the family. Merchant marine records from the National Archives show that, at eighteen or nineteen, he was third wireless operator on the Blue Funnel passenger ship *Ascanius*, bound for Australia. He sailed on other ships of the same line with names drawn from Greek myths – *Pyrrhus*, *Eurybates*, *Nestor* – all to Australia or the Far East. Having tired of the sea after rounding the world several times (he was seasick at the beginning of every voyage), he disembarked at Perth on the west coast of Australia and trekked on horseback across the Nullarbor Plain to South Australia and Sydney. There, the story goes, by building a wireless transmitter and sending a signal farther across the Pacific than any other competitor, he won a job – as head of the wireless telegraph station on Vila, in the New Hebrides, an island group 1,000 miles off the north-east coast of Australia. On the island he met and married Noel, daughter of wealthy Sydney hoteliers, and widow of a French plantation owner. Apart from holidays, including one to Britain at the time of the coronation of Queen Elizabeth when he received an award in recognition of his service, he spent the rest of his life in his tropical paradise. A Christmas card from Les, Noel and their children shows their home, a bungalow in a clearing, with tall tropical trees bending behind. It is long and low with a steeply pitched roof extended into a kind of awning that spreads shade over a terrace. Servants attended to their needs. Colonial ownership of the islands was shared between Britain and France and the uncle whom I met briefly spoke English, with what seemed to me an American accent, but of course it was Australian, and fluent French of the kind spoken in Marseille, from where most of his colleagues and friends on the island came. This linguistic peculiarity, we were told, saved him and Noel from being gulled or worse in a bar in Marseille during their European trip. They overheard two men discussing, in what the rogues assumed was impenetrable patois, how they might take advantage of these well-dressed foreigners – until Les stopped their plotting with a few well-chosen words in the same vernacular, at which they immediately became friendly and paid for drinks.

Thirty years before the Loves arrived in Newbridge, it had been a quiet hamlet with 'only two or three small collieries'. In 1876 the mine that later became known as Celynen South began producing coal on a far greater scale: in 1896, 1,600 men were employed there. It is highly likely that my grandfather worked in Celynen South, though no longer as a 'hewer of coal'. He had become an 'underground repairer', for this was how he described his employment at the 1901 Census. Between shifts, repairers attended to damaged tracks along which drams were hauled, brattices (wood or heavy cloth partitions that directed air for ventilation underground), pit props, and machinery where it was in place, indeed, everything necessary to keep the pit workings and access to them safe. It was a vital role and needed men experienced in working underground, capable, among other considerations, of judging the condition of the roof beneath which miners laboured. Repairers often worked as a team employed by a contractor who negotiated a fee for the job with the colliery management. For John Love it proved a valuable learning experience.

My mother began her education at the age of three. I believe she attended the Constables William James and Enoch Parry Board School where in 1901 (according to *Kelly's Trade Directory*) there were 482 pupils, including 150 infants. The school was situated approximately halfway between Newbridge and Crumlin, the next village, about a mile farther up the valley. There was another school nearby in the other direction, but she recalled an event that suggests she spent her infant schooldays not far from Crumlin. A man, she said, fell – or jumped – 200 feet from the railway viaduct at Crumlin into an inn yard below. Until 1964, when the Beeching railway closures made it redundant, it was the highest railway viaduct in Great Britain, third highest in the world. It would have been clearly visible from the school, and the horror of the falling man left a strong impression on her.

I have learned that people moved quite frequently in search of work, or better returns for their labour. I think my mother's father, having seen at Celynen South how underground repair work was contracted out and how the business was run, and confident he had the necessary knowledge and skill, decided to try his luck in the same line – not in Newbridge, but at a pit in another valley where an opening existed for a newly formed repair team. Sometime between 1905 and 1908, he brought his family to Clydach Vale – the valley of the Nant Clydach, a tributary of the river Rhondda, which it meets at Tonypandy. There, at the Cambrian Colliery, John Love set himself up as a 'colliery contractor', for that was his occupation when he registered the birth of his third son,

Gordon, in September 1907. Their first new home was near the top of the valley at Park Terrace, alongside the Taff Vale Railway, but they soon moved again, a few hundred yards further up to 70 Howard Street (perhaps to a larger house) overlooking the colliery. It was a huge mine, employing about 4,000 men, with railway sidings for 840 coal wagons. In March 1905, not long before my grandfather arrived there, thirty-three were killed in an explosion underground. It was a terrible reminder of the dangers of coal mining and the importance of measures to minimise risk, in which repairers had a large part to play.

By the time of the 1911 Census another child had been added to the family. Cyril was born in 1909. On one of our gossipy afternoons, sitting by the fire in the pub kitchen, Joan told me he was not the child of my grandmother, but of her daughter Winifred. Where my sister gathered this intelligence I have no idea; no one else ever mentioned it to me. Furthermore, she alleged that Winnie's liaison, with an unknown man, occurred in the ecstasy of religious revival. As with other stories she told, I think this was designed to shock. And I was shocked. The Evan Roberts revival, which set the Rhondda and most of Wales aflame, was a phenomenon of 1904–5 and does not fit the chronology, so the final colourful flourish of her tale may be an invention, but that did not invalidate the rest of the story. It was many years before I took the trouble to obtain a copy of Cyril's birth certificate. There, indeed, was proof: he was the son of Winifred May Love, but the name of his father is not given. Cyril was only two years younger than Gordon and was assimilated into the family. Winnie married Tom Woodgate in 1915, but Cyril was her only child.

Uncle Cyril, who was actually my cousin, was different from the other children brought up by my Love grandparents. I remember him coming home on leave during the war. Whereas his ostensible brothers were men of medium height at best (when he joined the merchant navy, Leslie was five feet six inches), he was tall – and lean, dark and handsome. He then wore a pencil moustache of the kind favoured by Hollywood heroes of the time, like Errol Flynn, and the uniform of the royal marines. He was a real commando. Though it seems highly unlikely, I have an obstinate recollection that he had a rifle with him. Joan knew him well and I believe had a childhood crush on him. She told me of his strange command over animals, how he had a pet spider with golden eyes that came when he called, and would carry a snake inside his shirt. There were also stories of his success with women. 'Love by name and love by nature,' he said, according to Joan, and went courting with a rug over his arm. I have a photograph of him when he was probably in his late teens, a lanky type with deep, dark eyes, very relaxed and suave, like a dancer. He went to dances where other young men saw him as a threat and was frequently in fights over girls. Joan told me that for some slight, real or imagined, he was taken up a back lane by a local policeman to be taught a lesson, but gave better than he got. After the war, he too lived in Barry, and was pursued hard by Peggy, whom I remember faintly as tense and ageing. Eventually he gave in and they were married in 1947, but not happily, because he continued to be attractive to other women. She once stabbed him in the shoulder. I do not remember seeing him properly again after that wartime encounter at the house in Glamorgan Terrace. The records say he died in Bournemouth in 1985.

Mary Jane Love was head of the household at 70 Howard Street at the national census on Sunday, 2 April 1911. With her were nine children, Winnie, the eldest, aged eighteen, Cyril, the youngest, just two. Her husband was not there. On the same day John Love was lodging with a married couple named Jones in Scotch Row, Gilfach Goch. His absence from the family home was almost certainly due to troubles in the mines, for he had arrived in Clydach Vale at about the time D. A. Thomas was establishing the Cambrian Combine. In the 1910–11 strike, those out of work had dole of seven shillings and sixpence a week for a limited period, then nothing. Forced to rely on the charity of others, Cambrian Clydach Vale miners gave out leaflets, 'Please Help the Unemployed', and sang in the streets:

> We are colliers from the Rhondda,
> Locked out of work at Clydach Vale,
> And it will surely make you wonder
> *When you've listened to our tale ...*
>
> When they introduced Conveyors
> Half our wages then they stole,
> Now they say the Pits aren't paying,
> And they have thrown us on the dole ...
>
> Kind friends, we do not ask for pity,
> Assistance is the thing we need,
> Cast out of work to starve with hunger
> Through the owners' selfish greed ...

I suspect John Love was not entirely sympathetic to their cause. As a contractor, he had set himself apart from them, and while they were on strike there was no work for him. With a wife and nine children to house and feed, he sought employment in Gilfach Goch. It is about ten miles by road from Clydach Vale to Gilfach, but less than a mile over the mountain, and over the mountain, I am sure, is the way my grandfather went. On census day he had left his home and family after what was probably a meagre Sunday dinner and tramped to Gilfach. There he lodged with the Joneses in Scotch Row, ready for work the next morning, as a miner once more, at one of the collieries not in the Combine and unaffected by the strike. He would not have been the only man to put care for wife and children above principle and take that mountain route. Perhaps the only question for them was how they might be received by erstwhile workmates and employers when the strike was over.

My mother gave me two memories of her life in Clydach Vale. She was twelve at the time of the strike and probably saw a great deal of the unrest, poverty and misery that accompanied it, but the only incident she recalled was witnessing a squad of tall policemen marching along a path flanked by a wall and strikers on top of the wall kicking out at the helmeted heads as they passed. The other memory was of the day in March 1910 when, without warning, an enormous volume of water dammed unseen in an abandoned drift mine on the hillside above the terraces overlooking the Cambrian Colliery burst out in a great flood. The deluge and boulders it had torn out of the mountain crashed through houses directly in their path, carved a valley across the school yard beyond, and flooded the girls' and infants' schools. It was fortunate that a shift had just ended at the pit and men were making their way home from work. They hauled timber and ladders to the windows of classrooms and pulled the children out. This my mother remembered, and being thrown over the torrent that crossed the yard to waiting arms the other side. She did not tell me three people were killed in the smashed houses and three of the schoolchildren drowned. Finally, the lower boundary wall of the school collapsed and the waters escaped into the Clydach stream and away.

It was some time before I realised that John Love was not the only absent family member at the time of the 1911 Census. Hubert, the oldest boy, was also missing. Eventually I found him entered as a 'Visitor' with a family named Hoare at Church Road, Newbridge, a neighbouring street close to Thorne Avenue, where the Loves had lived. They were clearly old friends. That Martha Hoare also came from Somerset may have been a reason for their closeness. Hubert, born in 1900, was still at school in 1911. If the Hoares were prepared to put him up, it was perhaps sensible to allow him to continue his education in Newbridge, where there was already a well-established county secondary school. I remember him smartly dressed, with a walking stick and a heavy limp, but a small man, hardly bigger than my mother or Aunty Lil, who were the smallest of his sisters. He had been disabled in an accident, one of the more remarkable stories I heard from my mother when I was a boy.

I cannot say where the events occurred – Newbridge, Clydach Vale or Gilfach Goch – for in and around all three were many abandoned mines, very few of which had been made safe. In my mother's story, Hubert and his brother took their small dog for a walk on the mountain. I had always assumed the other was daredevil Cyril, but he would have been a baby, so it was probably Leslie, who was only two or three years younger. They came across an old shaft, just like the one I knew at Penrhiwfer, easily accessible to anyone unwise enough to take the risk, and in some boyish foolery the dog fell into the pit. It is not difficult to imagine their anxiety and guilt as they came home without the dog. But however bad that had been, much worse followed when the two boys were in bed together and one of them became sure he could hear the dog whimpering down in the darkness. Sleep was impossible, so they rose, dressed and crept out, back to the uncovered shaft. There, leaning over and calling out to the dog, Hubert fell. He would have fallen to his death but for the chance of hitting an obstruction some dozen feet down, where he lay in agony until his brother raised the alarm and men came. He was brought up alive, although he never again walked properly.

Hubert was clever and good company, but could be a troublemaker. I was told he was a close friend of Jack Parry, a burly young man with pugilistic skills, who later became chairman of the Con Club and, at the price of a good night out paid for by a parliamentary candidate, found brief fame on record as a 'working man Conservative'. He and Hubert often went round the pubs together, from time to time raising drinking money by selling raffle tickets in bars for non-existent poultry. Hubert was known to start arguments that would lead to quarrels and end in altercations which Jack would settle with his fists. This kind of wildness ended when he married Gwyneth. For some time they lived down in the City. They had two children, beautiful Lovis and Graham. Hubert died in Haverfordwest when he was forty-five.

I don't know when my mother's family moved to Gilfach, except that it was after 1911. Nor do I know where they lived then, though it may well have been at 42 High Street, my mother's address when she married. At some time they moved to the house in Glamorgan Terrace, which, as I have said, Mama Love subsequently shared with Aunty Lil and Uncle Percy. I would visit occasionally, in my recollection always at teatime, when we ate toast and sardines, which I never had at home. Uncle Percy liked books; perhaps weeks of essential bed rest to get over bouts of pneumonia disposed him to be a reader. He did not possess a large library, but gave me two books that I have still: *How Much Do You Know?* which was packed with general knowledge questions and answers I read over and over, and *The Faber Book of Welsh Short Stories*, which eventually meant a great deal to me.

Whenever the Loves first came and wherever they settled in the valley, I am sure the six daughters caused a stir, because they were handsome and full of life – as they were still when I was a boy. They had so much to talk about and there was always laughter in the telling. They must have had jobs before they were married. Uncle Cyril's birth certificate reveals that Winnie was a 'draper's saleswoman'. Muriel recalls my mother saying she had been a milliner. Aunty Bernice became a 'pupil teacher', staying on at school after her thirteenth birthday to help with the teaching of younger pupils. Those ambitious to become qualified teachers would have served five probationary years in this way before sitting an examination for entry into training college. I do not know how long Bernice persevered with her probation, but I am sure she did not proceed to college. I have no idea how Lilian, Annie and Cissie might have been employed. When I knew them all three were married. I visited Cissie's home in Barry once. I don't know her husband's name or the names of their two teenage sons, but there was a shed in the garden that housed a half-size billiard table – that I remember. Aunty Annie, with the ready smile that crinkled her eyes, married Bill Harvey and kept a corner greengrocer's shop at a crossroads, opposite a small park in Cadoxton, Barry. Once or twice I spent holidays with them, sharing a double bed and chamber pot with their son, Colin, an only child, who was a little younger than I. Aunty Annie told me that the big boxes of Fyffes bananas they received direct from vessels at Barry Dock occasionally contained huge hairy spiders from the West Indies.

My mother was highly skilled at needlework of all kinds, during her later years making exquisitely embroidered tablecloths edged with finely crocheted lace. When I look back it does seem odd that, although I was very close to her, I know so little of her younger days. She went to dances, she told me, where the men always wore white gloves to protect their partners' dresses. Perhaps she met Tom Adams at a dance. Photographs of him at the time reveal a young man dressed as fashionably in the Edwardian style as Valleys outfitters could manage, and he went around with a group of friends, probably to dances and other social functions. In any case, the upper part of the village – streets of terraced houses strung along the valley slopes close to the mines – was not a big area. If only by sight, every face was known and familiar. My mother's was a face that must have attracted many glances. The only photograph I have of her as a young woman is a head and shoulders studio portrait against a dark, featureless background, perhaps intended for mounting in an oval frame. She is wearing a simple pale-coloured dress with a low collar, buttoned at the front almost to the throat, and she is looking over her left shoulder. So far as I can tell, she has light brown hair, quite short, brushed into a careless fringe, and then there is a short straight nose, and a wide mouth, which may be about to smile, and the most exquisite eyes. I can easily understand why my father fell for her, and fell forever. They were my mother and my father. To my childish perception they were as they had always been. It is only now, looking back down the long perspective of the years that I try (and fail) to recreate them as they were when young and first in love.

On 5 June 1920 they were married at St David's Church, Tonyrefail, also then the parish church of Gilfach Goch. Dats and Mama's brother Leslie, soon to go overseas, signed the register as witnesses. When my sister Joan was born in February 1921 and Barbara in November 1922, they were living at 142 High Street, perhaps with Aunty Julia and Uncle Will. My sisters gave the impression that the only home they had known was with Mam and Dats and I believe my parents moved there when the children were small, perhaps because Joan was a sickly child who needed a great deal of care. This too is conjecture: I know as little of the early years of Tom and Edith's married life as I know of their youth.

My parents were never young to me. When I was born in 1934, my father was thirty-eight, my mother thirty-seven, and by the time I was able consciously to look about me, most of what was light and easy in their lives had passed. My mother and I always talked a great deal and, before I could read for myself, she read to me. I have strong memories of sunny days sitting on the corrugated roof of the coalhouse, which was low on the garden side, reading comics, *The Dandy* and *The Beano*. We were there one day when a biplane flew low and slowly over the house so that you could see the pilot in the cockpit clearly and, to our intense surprise, a man standing on the wing holding on to one of the support struts. We conspired together to bury the small biscuit tin full of lead shot, which she thought were bullets. And I remember taking the pins from her hair and combing it gently. She loved playing the piano. We had a collection of sheet music and often I stood by her side turning the pages when she nodded. Her favourite piece was 'Autumn' by Cécile Chaminade. We had a lot of popular ballads too, including some from the Edwardian era, which she may have brought from her parents' home. As she played I sang in an undistinguished treble – 'We'll Gather Lilacs', 'Jealousy', 'The Anniversary Song', 'White Christmas' and so on. Through my school days she shined my shoes and cut my nails, even when I was old enough to do both for myself. Once, when she was in hospital, I noticed my fingernails needed cutting and felt suddenly, with a keen pang, that I was truly bereft. How trivialities sometimes bring home the consciousness of loss.

Bernice, Annie, Winnie and Cissie, my mother's sisters, seem larger than life in my memory. I was told that when I was very young I would sometimes be brought down from bed to entertain them with my infant chatter. Bernice lived with Uncle Reg at the pub nearby and occasionally one or two of the others would come up from Barry. Together they brimmed with merriment and seemed always ready for singing and dancing. Aunty Bernice was a great one for kicking up her legs. From time to time during the war years, on such occasions, drinks would be brought in from the Con Club just across the road, for Mr Davies, the club steward, and his wife were also invited. Having gone to bed earlier, I would wake to the noise of talk and laughter and the clink of glasses, and singing round the piano rising in gusts as the front room door opened and closed. And then there was usually a knock on the front door, a persistent knock, and Sid Vaughan, George and Trevor's father, would be there, already tipsy and attracted by the dim light through our blackout curtains. He was not tall, but big bellied with a round ill-shaved, red face and small eyes. He was a wet smoker and usually had a strand or two of tobacco stuck to his lips. I was often in the Vaughans' house and saw how sadly put upon was his gentle wife. But, maudlin in drink, Sid would extol her as 'the fairest flower that ever grew' and insist on singing 'Thora', a melancholy song for candle-lit Edwardian parlours, with jowls quivering and tears streaming:

I stand in a land of roses,
But I dream of a land of snow,
Where you and I were happy,
In the years of long ago.
Nightingales in the branches,
Stars in the magic skies,
But I only hear you singing,
I only see your eyes.
Come, come! come to me Thora,
Come once again and be
Child of my dream, light of my life,
Angel of love to me!

This is a very old memory, of a time when my mother often played the piano, while she had feet to press the pedals, without which, she said, it was not worth playing.

With the war came Barbara's marriage, the loss of her sailor husband and the birth of Leigh, her handicapped child. And with the war came the evacuee teachers, Miss Chaney and Miss Froggatt. They were given the back room, where I was not allowed to disturb them, and the bedroom above and, having handed over their ration books, full board. My mother usually made a small rice pudding for their dessert and if I was lucky I could scrape off the sweetish, milky singed edge of pudding from the enamel dish. The teachers came from Chatham. They were the assistant staff of a small girls' elementary school evacuated en masse to Gilfach. (The headteacher, Miss Bailey, was billeted elsewhere in the valley.) They were with us for a year at least, perhaps longer, and became good friends. After they returned home, Barbara wrote to them regularly, I suppose until they died. Although in their case it was born of the circumstances of the war, my parents having two teachers as lodgers echoes the arrangement Mam and Dats had thirty years before. I wonder now how we accommodated Miss Chaney and Miss Froggatt for they had one bedroom, Mama and Dada another, Barbara and her baby the third, while I had the smallest room over the hall. Where, then, did Joan sleep, before she married in 1944? It could only have been managed if she worked nights in the factory and slept during the day.

In all my boyhood I do not remember my mother being well and during the war years her health deteriorated. She had pain in her legs that made walking difficult. From time to time, when I was eight or nine, I would walk with her down the road to the pub kept by Aunty Bernice and Uncle Reg, a merry social drinker with a beacon nose and brittle bones. She didn't sit in the bar, which would have been highly unusual at the time, but in the kitchen where Bernice would join her for a chat if it wasn't too busy. The walk was little more than a hundred yards but she leaned on my arm and we stopped frequently to let the pain subside before she could go on. A doctor had told her she suffered from neuritis, for which he could do nothing. She took Phensic tablets, which claimed to relieve the pain. We bought them in little yellow packs at Joe Bacchetta's corner shop.

Some time before I was born, she had suddenly become completely blind. This too, specialists said, was neuritis, inflammation of the optic nerve, the causes of which remain a mystery. Mercifully, after some weeks, her vision returned. On holiday in the United States during the 1980s, long after her death, I chanced upon a medical book at the house where we were staying with friends, in which I found a reference to optic neuritis suggesting smoking as a possible cause. It seems to fit what I remember and what has become known of the pernicious effects of the cigarette habit. My mother had been a smoker from an early age and, finding that cigarettes alleviated, however slightly, the constant pain in her legs, she smoked more and more. At night she would sit at the side of the bed with her feet on the cold linoleum-covered floor for a moment's respite. She described a feeling as of a thick, knotted cord being drawn through her legs.

Eventually, it became obvious that her legs were patterned with red blotches and one was wasting but I am not aware that any other medical opinion was sought. Hadn't she been told she was suffering from neuritis? All this while, she cooked on the open fire and Barbara kept the house clean as best she could, burdened as she was, as we all were, with Leigh, her sick child, whose demands increased. It wasn't until after the war that his father's death at sea was confirmed, and then, when he was five or six, a permanent place was found for him at Hensol Hospital. What remains with me from those times is that life carried on and that whenever I returned from school or play, my mother was in the kitchen, usually seated in the corner armchair beside the fire. At the time, I did not fully appreciate the constancy of her presence and her love, and at what cost it was given.

***

It cannot have been long after my father's return from hospital that my mother's health declined sharply. The condition of her legs worsened to such an extent that she barely walked at all and was in constant pain that no proprietary pills could touch. Since she could no longer climb the stairs, a bed was brought down to the back room. As I look back, I think it may be possible that her disability helped persuade Dr Moody-Jones, our GP, that Barbara's son Leigh should be sent to an institution. Whether or not that was the case, he spent the rest of his short life in Hensol, leaving Barbara free to nurse Mama, and occasionally in the evening to help behind the bar at the Con Club, where my father was a member of the committee. On one such occasion, she attracted the attention of Emrys Simons, a solicitor from Tonyrefail, who was keen to establish himself as a Tory activist, perhaps a future candidate, by persuading the membership to vote Conservative – a hopeless task, since the membership was, with the odd exception, staunchly socialist. He came over the road to see my mother, a tall man with thinning auburn hair, a thick moustache of the same colour, and an enviably sociable manner. This was almost certainly during the run-up to the general election of February 1950, won by Labour. I was fifteen, in the first year of sixth form A-level studies. By this time Mama remained day and night in the front room, propped in a corner of the settee with a shawl or blanket tucked around her. Her wretched state did not deter Emrys. He was always merry with her, at first calling her Ede, as my father did, but very soon, Chuter, borrowed from the Labour politician James Chuter Ede, and she was always cheered by his presence. Also he brought her cigarettes, for now she smoked incessantly. A gift box of fifty Sobranie from Emrys she finished overnight. One day she showed me a hole, an ulcer, which had suddenly appeared on the shining, swollen ankle of what she called her 'good' leg – not to shock, I am sure, but to prepare me, because a dreadful odour of rot rose from it. The leg was gangrenous and there could be no delay. It was amputated at once at Cardiff Infirmary. Within a very short time she returned to hospital and the other leg was removed.

After some weeks in a convalescent home at St Mellons, east of Cardiff, she returned home. Her bed was set up near the windows in the front room where there was the possibility of seeing a little of the outside world, but she had no strength and little interest beyond the family. The wound in the stump of the first amputation refused to heal and it seemed she must remain bedridden. She was, I believe, saved by what seemed an unaccountable craving for fruit. Most foods were still rationed and fruit of any kind was scarce, but by the happiest of coincidences pomegranates from Palestine began to arrive at the Co-op. My mother had an appetite for them that gradually extended to other foods. Slowly strength returned and the wound began to heal. After pomegranates came grapefruit, and when visitors to her bedside said, 'Why don't you try Mackeson's Milk Stout – it's just the thing to build you up', she did and was surprised to find it palatable, and then grew to like it. People began to say that she looked well, and we agreed: she had no legs but appeared in better health than I could ever remember.

A wheelchair was provided and for a while we pushed her from room to room. There was no question of going outdoors, although the front path was concreted to allow it. She began to propel herself and, more quickly than we had dared to hope, she became independent and took her place at the hub of the household once more, in the kitchen. Disabled people are sometimes said to be confined to a wheelchair; my mother was liberated by hers. An electric stove allowed her to cook for us, and a top-loading washing machine next to the Belfast sink meant she could supervise the washing. As much as it is possible to do from a wheelchair, she did. When she was fully capable of managing on her own, Barbara began working regularly in Glyn Jones's shop selling electrical goods.

I wrote home weekly throughout my six years in Aberystwyth, long letters describing all that went on. I know they were read avidly. When I was home on vacation my mother was keen to know about the books I had been studying. She had left elementary school at thirteen, a common case in the 1900s, and had not been bookish – a great talker, but not a reader. It could not have been easy to find enough time or, later, relief from pain, to read. But, healthily and I believe, contentedly disabled, during my college years she began shadowing my English course, or at least the novels in it. She read Sterne, Defoe, Richardson, Fielding, Dickens: *Great Expectations* and *Tom Jones* were great favourites.

A new pattern of family life was established: Dada went to work early, catching the bus to Park Colliery or Cwm, Barbara bustled about cleaning and ensuring everything necessary was within reach before she went to the shop, and Mama kept house from her wheelchair. This was how things were when, one morning, Bob Wilkins knocked on the front door. Opening the door from the wheelchair presented physical problems. The design of the chair meant that a frontal approach to the high brass knob of the Yale lock was not possible; nor could it be reached from the side. But, by reversing to the door and reaching backwards above her head, it could be done. So my mother opened the door to find a stranger on the threshold, a breathless fat man with a red unshaven face, in a dirty overcoat almost to his ankles and a slouch hat, saying, 'Can I go through the back, Missis?'

'Why?'

'Well, I don't want the police to see me.'

Goodness knows what prompted my mother to invite the fugitive in, but soon he was sitting in the kitchen having a cup of tea and explaining himself. He was, indeed, trying to evade the police, because he had a pocketful of betting slips. His job was to visit pubs and billiard halls, or simply stand on street corners, collecting the bets of men, usually, who regularly gambled on horse racing. He was employed as a bookie's runner, an illegal activity, although you could bet on racecourses or by telephone if you had an account with a bookmaker. From time to time it would be Bob's turn to be summonsed for the offence. He would be intercepted by the police and the betting slips confiscated. In due course he would appear before the magistrates' court in Llantrisant and be fined £5. The bookie would pay the fine. This was an arrangement he understood very well; it happened regularly. Yet he persisted with the charade of flight, often by the stratagem he had adopted with my mother, which entailed entering a house by the front door, leaving immediately through the back and running along the lane at the rear into another terrace and so away. If the police were determined they would, anyway, simply turn up at his lodgings. There were usually spurious betting slips available to serve as evidence.

My mother found this intriguing. She wanted to know how you placed a bet and how you would know if you had won or lost. Bob showed her the cards of the day's race meetings in the newspaper, explained betting odds and recommended each way cross doubles. This seemed harmlessly amusing and was certainly a change. Bob, who knew a good deal about racing form, suggested a few likely horses and she risked a shilling or two under his guidance. He returned the following morning with her modest winnings and over a cup of tea they discussed that day's runners and riders and my mother placed another bet. So began a routine that continued until the 1960 Betting and Gaming Act introduced betting shops and cleared the street of characters like Bob who brought colour to a drab post-war world. By then my mother knew enough about racing to make her own selections and she continued to win rather more often than she lost, though never very much. The televising of horse racing brought her another dimension of pleasure. If a meeting was broadcast in the afternoon, she would inevitably be found in the front room watching closely, with newspaper and racing form book on the table beside her.

The loss of her legs transformed my mother. It was as though a great burden had been lifted from her. Although the phantom limb sensation occasionally bothered her, she no longer lived in pain. She had not been used to going out for many years before the amputations and was happy afterwards to be confined to the house, where there were few domestic chores beyond her reach and ability. When they were done she carried on with her knitting or embroidery, usually, if it were dry and warm, in the doorway of the back room where she could feel the sun and look out over the garden. An abiding memory of this time is seeing her with two Siamese cats stretched asleep across her lap among skeins of fine coloured silks, undisturbed as she stitched or crocheted. At supper time, about ten o'clock, she would begin the flagon of Ind Coope's Nut Brown Ale that Dada had brought earlier from the Con Club, and while we ate, she would drink and talk until the beer was finished before wheeling herself to bed in the back room.

In 1947, as soon as he was able, my father joined the National Coal Board Principal Superannuation Scheme, as I assume did all mineworkers. By the time of his retirement in

1961, his fourteen years of pensionable service had earned him a pension of £100 17s payable in monthly instalments of £8 8s, and a lump sum of £302 11s. It was not much to show for fifty years' work, but without nationalisation there would have been nothing. And he continued to receive compensation for the injury to his right hand. There was little enough to spare for maintaining the house, so he carried on doing what he could. While the house became a little shabbier life within it seemed unchanged; my mother and father, though older, the same as ever.

That was, of course, illusory. My mother died quite suddenly in 1966. She had enjoyed almost twenty pain-free years in which she resumed her place as true head of the household around whom all activity revolved and, because she was confined to a wheelchair, had found unexpected pleasures in needlework, reading, gambling on the horses, a few glasses of beer accompanied by conversation, and television, which brought a glimpse of the wider world indoors to her. As a widower, my father began cooking dishes that he recalled from his childhood. I knew he enjoyed the butchers' stalls in Cardiff Market, the array of cuts, the variety of offal, the sausages and cooked meats. If he had ever visited France he would have had more pleasure sampling charcuteries than strolling promenades. To Barbara's surprise, he turned his hand, his left hand, to almost forgotten delicacies like brawn. Who knows where this might have led? – had he not discovered a motorbike and with it a project.

The bike was a 1919 AJS, registration number L7473, which he had glimpsed mouldering in a neighbour's back garden. He and Joan's husband Tommy bought it for £10, £5 each, and hauled it to the house. It was a primitive monster with tyreless spoke wheels and a long petrol tank that had flat sides and top, all badly corroded. But my father knew at once that the vital parts of the engine were intact, and saw a challenge. Without the shed as a garage, he did the next best thing: he brought it into the back room, virtually empty since

Mama's death. There he could work on the machine at any hour of the day or night he had a mind to. Alone, one-handed, he sandpapered the rusted metal to a gleam, bought (when he could afford them) a new seat and tyres, re-painted the petrol tank and the AJS insignia. Then he took the engine apart, cleaned it inside and out, and reassembled it. Muriel and I and our boys, Nicholas and Jonathan, were by this time living in Caerleon, less than an hour away from Gilfach, and saw the bike gradually transformed. We were there when he put a gallon of petrol in the tank and tried to kick it into motion for the first time in thirty years. It was at first reluctant, but eventually it coughed and started in a cloud of black smoke and with a roar that sent the boys scurrying out of the room. With some difficulty, a few days later, it was carried out to the garden for photographs. I have one beside me. My father is seated on the bike. He grips the handlebar with his left hand, the damaged right out of sight on the far side. He is looking at the camera and smiling.

My father died suddenly, in his sleep, in April 1971. I do not remember my mother's funeral, a case, perhaps, of psychological block, but I remember his. At the service in the crematorium at Glyn Taff, I was surprised when the chapel filled behind me with men from Gilfach Goch who had come by special bus, and when they sang together for him it was almost more than I could bear.

My parents were not demonstrative in their love for one another, but that it was deep love and abiding commitment I have no shadow of doubt. For as long as my mother lived they shared a bed. Both were disabled, but I never heard either complain or grieve for their loss. My father cursed under his breath with frustration when the lump of misshapen flesh that had been his right hand could not be made to work as he wanted, but he didn't mope about it. My mother's disability meant that she couldn't use the bathroom or lavatory; access as an issue and a right of the disabled had not been thought of. For some of her most basic needs she required my father's help.

It was never spoken of. Preoccupied with my own interests, and away for much of the time from 1952, I floated above these domestic concerns, although I knew that 'slopping out' was part of the daily routine. I know, too, that my mother's will prevailed in all things. Her manner was never domineering, but she dominated the household, and my father deferred to her. Early and late, and forever, he would have done anything for her. That is just how things were.

Eleven

THE WELFARE PARK in Gilfach Goch is bounded on one side by a small patch of allotments. Running away more or less at right angles from the allotments is a street of pebble-dashed, semi-detached houses, Heol y Parc, and at right angles again, completing the open square, another street of semis, grey and in my recollection constantly in the shade, called Glannant. In one of the latter houses my cousin Bloom and his wife Megan brought up two daughters. At the end of this short road was the Squint, the colliery where my father worked. The farther edge of the park, opposite Heol y Parc, falls steeply away to the Ogwr Fach, the stream that near its source ran (perhaps still runs) red, but throughout my childhood divided the village, west from east, like a broad black thread. The park was the only horizontal surface of any size in the valley that was not occupied by collieries or slag heaps. Its creation probably required considerable earth-moving effort. The field where rugby, soccer and cricket are played, and where soon after the war gymkhanas were held and flamboyantly-attired marching jazz bands with buzzing gazookas competed, is heavy clay beneath a sparsely grassed surface, as those who play winter games know all too well.

The park entrance, near the allotments and the beginning of Heol y Parc, has tall, double ornamental gates that are normally locked, and a smaller, heavy wrought-iron gate in everyday use. To the left within the gates is a neatly grassed square edged with flower beds, and at its centre, on a low plinth, a slim four-sided clock tower with a weather vane on its pyramidal summit. It is built of bricks that have an unusual dull red hue, very like the bricks that you will see in villages in Flanders rebuilt after the destruction of the First World War. A brass plaque fixed to one side of the tower is the village's memorial to the fallen of the two world wars and later conflicts. In the second week of November the double gates are opened for the Remembrance Day parade, when wreaths of poppies are leaned against the tower. The plaque does not name individuals, but the British Legion preserves a board on which each is honoured in gilded lettering.

During the First World War, when some 273,000 Welshmen served in the forces and 35,000 died, Gilfach lost six of its sons. Among them was William Webber, a private in the 17th Battalion of the Welch Regiment, one of the battalions composed of men who were below the regulation height of five feet three inches, known as 'bantam battalions'. He came from Abercerdin Road and the language of the home was Welsh, and he was killed in Flanders on 5 September 1917, probably during the long, terrible Third Battle of Ypres.

There are many moving accounts of war in the trenches. One I return to was written by Ford Madox Ford, an Englishman (albeit of part-German ancestry) who, like William Webber, belonged to the Welch Regiment. It is not from his great four-volume sequence *Parade's End*, but written on the spot, in France. Ford enlisted in 1915 at the age of forty-two, and was commissioned as a second-lieutenant. After training in Wales, in July 1916 he sailed for France with the 9th Battalion, Welch Regiment. Before going to war he had felt an even-handed sympathy for all those involved, friend and foe alike, but experience altered him. He soon found he hated the Hun and wished them all dead, and cared with an extraordinary depth of feeling for the men of his battalion and those others of the Welch Regiment who served alongside them. One piece, originally written in French for *La Revue des Idées*, exemplifies this heightened comradely feeling. A vessel is carrying a boatload of Welch Regiment troops, eight hundred men and two hundred and fifty officers who had all come from South Wales [...] We had sung ... and sung ... and eaten our rations ... and sung ... and drunk the waters of the Seine ... and sung. And then, silence; and the ripples of the river whispering ... A large Red Cross steamer came down the river amidst a whirlwind of hurrahs ... And then silence ...

And suddenly one voice, coming from the bank ... shouted to us across the whispers of the water: 'Where do you go from?'

And with one voice, as in an enormous, Aristophanic laugh the boat replied:

"Pon ... ti ... pri ... ith!"

They would reach their destination at the height of the battle of the Somme.

Ford was fluent in German and French, but the language of the Tommies, over forty per cent of whom would probably have been Welsh speakers at that time, is alien to his ears, 'as if you were hearing ravens chatting'. More remarkably, when you think of the importance of communication in the ranks, '[s]everal thousand of them could not make themselves understood in English'. But –

[t]hey sing at all times and for all reasons; and they play football – at all times and for all reasons! It was the Welch Regiment that advanced at Etreux in 1914, kicking a football and shouting 'Stick it, the Welch'; and singing in chorus. [...] They sing like angels and the prophets ... and like men who are about to die [...] for in six days, the majority – the majority, alas! – of them would give their lives in Mametz wood.

In 'A Day of Battle', written 'in the Ypres salient: 15th Sep. 1916', he attempts to explain how a rational human being can keep going in the face of bombardment and terrible destruction, of bodies mangled or 'burst into mere showers of blood and dissolving into muddy ooze', and of his own expectation of imminent death. For him at least, the answer was concentration on the task in hand, especially as it involved 'hypnotic' responsibility for the lives of others. Here again, sympathy is reserved principally for his own battalion. He remembers individually:

> the wounded of my own Bn. that I have seen. The poor men, they come down from Pontypridd and Nantgarw and Penarth and Dowlais Works and they have queer, odd, guttural accents like the croaking of ravens, and they call every hill a mountain … and there is no emotion so terrific and so overwhelming as the feeling that comes over you when your own men are dead […] the little, dark, raven-voiced, Evanses, and Lewises, and Joneses and Thomases … Our dead!

These are Gilfach's dead: Frederick Jelleyman, lance-sergeant, of the 1st Battalion Welch Guards, killed in action 10 September 1916 on the Somme; Pte J. Rees of the Welch Regiment; George Fisher, a sergeant in the RAMC, died in Mesopotamia 31 August 1917; Robert Morgan of the Royal Welch Fusiliers, a rugby player of great promise, who was awarded the Military Medal, died on the battlefield in Flanders on 11 March 1918; Ivor Jenkins, a driver with the RASC, died 30 January 1918 on home soil.

The fact that many thousands of miners from south Wales enlisted in the first months of the war suggests that the list may be incomplete. It certainly lacks one famous name, for in recent years evidence has been found to show that George Prowse VC DCM was born in Gilfach Goch in 1886. He is linked also with Landore, Swansea, where he enlisted and where his widow resided, and Camerton in Somerset, where his father was living at the time of the hero's death. It seems likely the father, John Prowse, a miner, brought his family to Gilfach in the 1880s, so George, his second son, was born there and some time later returned to his home village. George Prowse, too, was a miner before he enlisted. He joined the Royal Navy but his active service was on land, first at Gallipoli and from 1916 in France. The several acts of courage early in September 1918 for which he received the Victoria Cross are almost beyond imagining, utterly heroic. Before the end of the month he lost his life at Anneux, a village just south of the road from Cambrai to Bapaume. It had been captured from the enemy in November 1917, and yielded to them again a few weeks later. The 63rd (Royal Naval) Division was in the force that retook it on 27 September 1918. During this latter action CPO Prowse was killed. He was awarded the Victoria Cross posthumously in November 1918.

The toll of the Second World War was far greater. Of 15,000 servicemen from Wales who died, thirty-six were from Gilfach: eighteen soldiers, nine from the RAF, eight seamen and one Marine. Two of the sailors who lost their lives went down with HMS *Repulse*, one of them my brother-in-law, Leighton. As a child I experienced the faintest shadow of the hollowness of loss that afflicted my sister and my parents, and now in remembrance I think of the pall that, for months and long years, hung over the families of the other thirty-five young men who did not return from the war.

Twelve

It is difficult for me to imagine the relationship between siblings born in the usual way quite close together. My own experience was so different, born twelve years after my sister Barbara, and almost fourteen after Joan. The children of my marriage, born in Bristol only fifteen months apart, differ quite markedly in appearance and temperament but, beyond infancy, they learned household and daily routines together, went to nursery school together, explored the garden and the wider outdoors in one another's company, had the same friends, came to know the network of relations, Muriel's and mine, at the same time. They have a common hoard of impressions of people and places, familiar points of reference they can recall and talk about together. They remember Barbara, having spent brief holidays in Tonyrefail with her and Glyn and, though they did not see as much of Joan and Tommy, have not forgotten the pub, known locally as The Bog, the hump-backed bridge into the car park, the garden of cropped grass and beaten earth bounded by stables, and that extraordinary flock of birds – chickens, ducks, geese, guineafowl and peafowl – that strutted and fluttered forward with voices raised to greet my sister whenever she came into the yard. Our boys can talk and remind one another about these things, whereas I shared nothing of the childhood experiences of my sisters, or indeed of the young married days of my parents, and almost nothing of my father's parents with whom they lived.

I grew up in a family much altered from that which my sisters had known, with parents no longer young and active, but staid, weighted with greater responsibility and, in my mother's case, in declining health. Moreover, my grandfather, who had built the security within which they all lived, and whom all loved, was no longer there. As I look back, the beginning of my life seems to coincide with the outbreak of the Second World War. I have no recollection of Joan from those early days. I wonder how that can be when we slept in the same house, doubtless ate meals together. It is the horses that bring her suddenly into my consciousness when I am eight perhaps, and even then she does not seem to be at home with us. It was only in her last decade or so that I began really to know her, when, widowed, she still kept the pub and I used to visit, perhaps a dozen times a year, to spend a couple of hours with her, talking by the fireplace in the kitchen, with the circle of dozing cats and dogs about us.

I had talked constantly with my mother, and with Barbara, but my father was not one to initiate conversation unless it served a specific purpose. It had been the same with Joan until those late years, after retirement had freed me for trips to Gilfach during weekdays, when the pub was usually closed in the afternoons because no one could be bothered to negotiate the rutted lane in search of a drink. Age difference had long been a barrier between us. A teenager when I was born, she resented the changes my infant presence entailed. I aroused no nascent maternal feelings in her. I got in the way; I was a nuisance. When young, she might well have been a tomboy; as a young woman she was hardy and tough-minded, able to hold her own among the rough, ragged boys and young men in the valley, the sort who rode wild and bareback, by the force of her personality and a readiness when provoked to lash out with whatever was to hand. In her seventies she would take a broom and belabour men who had transgressed the pub's code of etiquette and sweep them out of the door.

My parents could hardly have anticipated the development of a termagant (as she was, when occasion demanded) because she suffered a succession of serious childhood illnesses any one of which might have killed her. Her earliest memory, she told me, was of looking up at Mama and Dada weeping at the side of the cot where she lay, apparently dying. There were brushes with death later, much later, but she was blessed with a will to live and remarkable powers of recuperation, and saw them off, one after the other – almost all.

Her poor start in life might have accounted for her diminutive size, but genetic inheritance had something to do with it. Our mother was a little over five feet tall, one of the short, fine-boned members of a family that also included three sisters whose big-boned, handsome stature was unusual in a village where shortness was the norm. They were as tall as, or taller than, my father, who was of medium height for the times. My sister Barbara was much the same size as my mother; Joan, at barely four foot ten, made up by force of character for what she lacked in inches.

The expectation that she would ease the burden on my mother by helping to look after me, if only by taking me for a walk in the pram, was an immense irritation. 'If he needs a walk, I'll give him a walk' might have described her attitude. With a friend similarly encumbered by a young sibling, she introduced me to experiences that most babies are spared, like bumping over rough paths and down long flights of steps, and racing along uneven pavements. They let the prams roll downhill in the cemetery and chased after them, half-fearing, perhaps half-hoping for, a disaster. Of course, I remember nothing of this, though it might have left me somewhat apprehensive of the world. As I grew older, Joan tested my courage whenever she had the chance. Once, at the funfair in Porthcawl, she dared me to join her on the 'Dive Bomber', an invention of the devil, which consisted of a pair of revolving cockpits at the ends of long arms that swung over and over like weighted propellers. She didn't turn a hair, while I sat sick and petrified, hardly able to move when the machine stopped and we were released from the safety belts.

Joan left the elementary school at fourteen, whether to some sort of employment or a loose end I don't know, while Barbara, who 'passed the scholarship' in 1934, was among the first intake at the new grammar school in Tonyrefail that I later attended. This, perhaps, meant that, for a couple of years at least, Joan was conveniently placed to lend a hand about the house, while Barbara was at her lessons. There are many chasms, unbridgeable now, in my knowledge of what my parents and sisters were doing at various times, and this is one. I believe Barbara too left school at fourteen, without taking, or certainly without success in, the School Certificate. She had been given a set of stout, densely-worded encyclopaedias, still pristine when I turned their pages a decade later. It was as much encouragement as our parents (neither of whom had progressed beyond the elementary school) could give – but she, not surprisingly, had made nothing of them.

The war changed everything. In February 1939, or soon after, when Joan was eighteen, she began working at the Royal Ordnance factory in Bridgend. This participation in the war effort, daily or perhaps nightly (I am unsure of the shift patterns she worked), probably accounts for my inability to place her in the house when I think of those times. I am sure she had no difficulty adapting to challenging routines and the hazards of working with explosives. It was no doubt her wish, and might have seemed a good idea for someone daily employed with noxious substances, to go riding at weekends. So it came about that Bonny, a pretty bay Welsh-mountain pony, the first of our horses, was bought for her from one of the Griffiths clan up the top of the valley, flatcart purveyors of greengrocery and Friday fish. Younger Griffiths kin and their daredevil pals rode the ponies when they were released from the shafts.

Jockey-sized and fearless, Joan took to the saddle as though bred to it from infancy, though not with Bonny, because the little bay disappeared on the day we bought her. We did not have a stable. That wasn't a problem, old man Griffiths told my father: 'We let them out on the mountain in the evening and, when we want them in the morning, we go up with a bucket with a few carrots in it, or an apple or two, and they come soon enough.' That seemed an easy solution, and after showing the pony off at the back gate, for my mother to admire through the window, and Joan's first ride, Bonny was stripped of saddle and bridle and released on to the mountain above our house. The next morning there was no sign of her. Had she overnight strayed up the valley to her usual patch? No. She was not among the Griffiths's horses – or anywhere else in the valley. When it became clear she was not to be found we bought Betsy and, having learned a hard lesson, rented the old, neglected stables that belonged to the Glamorgan Hotel.

It is about this time that out of the mist and chaos of early memories some clarity emerges. Betsy I remember well (as I do Bonny, but later and for a different reason). She was a glowing chestnut of twelve-and-a-half hands, with a refined white blaze between her eyes and uneven white socks at the front. And she was a riding horse that had been little used for pulling a cart or trap. Joan rode whenever she could, and if she came off once or twice in the early days, she only cursed herself and got back on. The stables were separated from the hotel, 'the Glam', a large, gaunt, wholly undistinguished building, by a steep path cobbled with pale pebbles, over which shod hooves scraped and clattered. Up or down, on this path the horses were led, and turned in at a door set in a high wall. To the right along the narrow yard behind the wall and through another door was our stable, where we had three stalls with mangers and hayracks over. In the third, inner stall we stored bales of straw for the brick floor, and hay, chaff and oats for feed. A stiff tap gave running water. I lacked the strength to lift a full bucket up to its place in the manger, though the horses sucked water from one I filled and dragged towards them over the floor. Nor could I reach the manger with their feed, but I learned from my father how to offer titbits held flat on the palm of my hand. The velvet snuffling of a horse as it takes half an apple from your open palm is not easily forgotten.

I remember rising early on winter mornings and, in darkness still, walking up Glamorgan Terrace and along the broad dirt track at the back of High Street, the mountain a great gloom on the right. Hearing our approach, the horses would be restless, ready for breakfast. They always seemed to me huge in the dim yellow glow when my father switched on the light. Forking the soiled straw to add to the heap at the back of the yard was my job, then stiffly brushing the deeply-incised, diamond-patterned purple bricks of the floor. I was always aware of the horses watching me sidelong as I brushed around and beneath them. Without pause in the rhythmic munching of oats and chaff they turned their eyes on me, showing a wide rim of white. One might bend a back leg so that the front edge of the hoof alone touched the ground, poised as if to kick out, though it never did. Rhona, a tall roan mare, the answer to Joan's dream of a real hunter for putting at hedges and fences, would move gradually as I swept and, if she could, trap me between her great swollen belly (for she was in foal) and the wooden partition of the stall. She knew I was afraid of her and did it to tease. This labour earned me the right to ride, but I was not greatly taken with the idea, though I did occasionally, hoping I might be seen by friends. But even on a small pony, it seemed a long way down to the ground.

I never rode with Joan, who had no patience with my ineptitude. My companion on these occasions was Ray, a boy of fifteen or so, the son of an impoverished, shiftless family who lived in a squalid house at the top of the valley. There was no shortage of work, but Ray's father, able-bodied though he was, turned up at the pit only when desperate for drinking money. The family lived much of the time on bread and condensed milk. Ray attached himself to Joan, a ragged squire, following wherever she determined to go. Joan saw how hungry he was, for food and human kindness. Occasionally she brought him to the house for something to eat, and gradually he became a regular caller. So it came about he was given a home by my parents and shared my bed: when I got up for school, Ray, whom my father had introduced to the routine and ethic of honest labour, and worked 'nights regular' in the pit, took my place. He lived with us until, at eighteen, he decided on National Service in the army.

Nine months had passed since Bonny's disappearance when suddenly she returned. She had been recognised by a Gilfach man on a farm near Glynogwr, a hamlet with an old New Inn and an older church, only a few miles from Gilfach, though in an unexpected direction. That she had strayed there does not say much for horse sense. The farmer said he had found her wandering on his land, had made enquiries about ownership and when no one claimed her had used her himself. He had abused the pony horribly, harnessing her to haul heavy loads and beating her when she could not. The news reached my father, who hastened to retrieve her. The farmer didn't yield easily: he had fed and housed the beast for the best part of a year. My father pointed to the pony's ribs and matted coat and weals, and mentioned the police.

She returned to us a wild thing, as though never broken, and contrived sooner or later to throw all who attempted to ride her, including Joan and Ray, who limped home from one attempt with a broken collarbone. When eventually she quietened and seemed amenable again, I was allowed to ride her. One day, I went, with Ray on Betsy for company (and just in case), along a familiar route up the broad black path known as The Rhiw that climbed the mountain the other side of the valley and looped around the farms, Hendre-ifan-goch, Bryn Chwith and Maendy, which lay over the crest. All went well until, on our return to the village, just as we reached the main road, we chanced upon a gang of children chasing one another brandishing sticks. Bonny took fright. I knew at once I was helpless, and there was nothing Ray could do. With a straight, flat quarter-mile of macadamised road ahead of her, she bolted. I hung on, my arms clamped around her neck until, blown, she was caught and held by the bridle inches from the plate-glass window of the Co-op shoe department. I was in no condition properly to see, far less thank, the man who held her until Ray came panting up. Fortunately there had been no traffic, as was usual in those days, when we regularly played football in the road while waiting for the school bus. Even so, I had been very lucky. Bonny might have been quietly sold after that, to what end I do not know; I did not miss her. I could sit a saddle well enough, but never felt in command of the horse – rather the reverse.

Late in life, when she was widowed, Joan set me a final equestrian test. In a field belonging to the pub she kept in retirement Pierrot, an ancient children's riding pony. He was in his late twenties, a diminutive grey with the wisdom of great age. 'Why don't you take the boys up to see Pierrot?' she suggested. She gave me a bucket with some titbits. 'Call him, he'll come,' she said. 'He's a lovely old thing.' I should have known better than to fall for it.

We went up to the field together and through the five-barred gate. Pierrot was grazing quietly fifty yards off but when I called and banged the bucket he started towards us, his old head nodding as he plodded forward. As he neared he seemed to see us more clearly and his pace quickened. He picked up his feet like a much younger horse, laid his ears back and bared his long, discoloured teeth. Even a small horse looks inordinately large when it gets close to you. The children scattered and with as much dignity as I could muster I put the bucket down and walked briskly back to the gate. I swear I heard snickering behind my retreating back. 'Did he come?' my sister said. 'Oh yes, he came. I left the bucket with him.' She smiled.

When she was free to do so, Joan rode Betsy or Rhona from early to late, hour after hour, over the mountains. She was small and dark, with huge blue eyes like our mother's. She had a kind of free-spirited beauty and the rough boys, riders since early childhood, admired her hardiness and spirit. They had showed her the ropes and taught her the routes across the moorland. On one occasion, she and Ray trekked as far as Neath – a long, lonely journey over the remote tops of the valleys. In a place of desolate solitude they came upon an extensive bog and saw in the midst of it the shattered fragments of a German warplane. Were the flyers still there, picked clean, they wondered, as they skirted the undulating waste of rushes, oil-tainted pools, and cotton grass.

One of her regular rides was to Llangeinor, not far away from Gilfach on the mountain overlooking the Ogmore Valley. We might still have had relatives there, because Dats's family had lived there when he was a boy, before they moved to Gilfach. Out of these journeys arose a friendship with members of the Llangeinor Hunt. Much later the Boxing Day meet of the hunt was regularly held at The Bog, when the car park would be full of horses, huntsmen and friendly hounds with tongues lolling and banner tails waving aloft. On summer visits I would sometimes find a brace of hounds that had been billeted with Joan for their summer holidays from the kennel, accepted by her own dogs and cats, wandering cheerfully among the domestic fowls in the yard. She loved animals, but without sentiment and mawkishness. She treated them well and expected them to do what they were told. Their multi-coloured variety and behaviours interested her. 'It's all sex and violence out there,' was her usual comment on the spring mating rituals. The competing voices of cockerels, ducks and geese could reach alarming volume, but the pub, down in its dip, half a mile from the road, was far enough from houses for even the unearthly yells of peacocks to seem suitably muted to her nearest neighbours. In the long empty days of her later years she viewed with amused detachment these gaudy birds with exquisite tails erect and rattling with lust, ganders chasing geese, and cockerels flying in pursuit of hens.

At odd times animals turned up on her doorstep, as though there were signs directing them, the sorts of mark tramps made that told fellow wayfarers where hospitality was to be found. It was not unusual to find a strange cat or dog in the group assembled by the fire in the kitchen, though the orphaned lamb caught out by winter, lying in the hearth blinking its amber eyes was a surprise – as was the turkey, which grew into an aggressive pink and purple-wattled cock commanding the entrance to the back door. She took them all in and dealt with them generously, even-handedly and firmly. I never saw a squabble among them.

In 1944, Joan married Tommy. He was in the forces. I heard the tale that he started in the RAF, but while training as a pilot in Canada crashed a precious plane and found himself transferred to the navy, where he was less likely to damage the war effort. True or not, he was certainly in the navy towards the end of hostilities, because he brought home an enormous naval duffel coat that he later persuaded me, reluctantly, to take in exchange for a donkey jacket I had bought in Aberystwyth. No chill wind penetrated that duffel, but it fell below my knees and weighed heavily on me. I was glad to sell it to a considerably taller fellow student. Tommy resumed his pre-war job as a Post Office telephone engineer, in which eventually he became hugely experienced and expert, and so continued until retirement. He drove the GPO crested green van in the same style as he walked, with swagger.

Tommy was short, sturdy and swarthy, with crinkled black hair and narrow, dancing dark eyes. He was quick, vigorous and assertive, perhaps too much like Joan for the match ever to have grown into calm companionship. My cousin Jean told me they had separated in the early days of marriage and for a time Joan lived in Llanelli with Aunty Julia and Uncle Will. Knowing the volatile nature of their personalities, it was not altogether surprising to hear of this rupture more than fifty years after the event.

I have one recollection of their wedding. Tommy's father was the Co-op milkman. From a covered cab at the front he commanded the four-wheeled milk wagon, painted pale brown and cream, rather like a large gipsy caravan, but with open sides, which was drawn by a splendid shire horse in matching colours. The horse knew the route and could have plodded the round without the least direction. Many ration coupons had been saved to furnish the reception, held at our house, but beyond that shared effort, the link with the Co-op, which did the catering, was all-important. Of bride, groom and ceremony I now see nothing, but chocolate éclairs filled with real cream remain in my memory.

They set up home in a small semi-detached house at the top of Thomas Street, that last row in the City, near the crossroads that is still the entrance and exit to the village. The house was more or less on the flat, before the street plunges steeply down to the fence bordering the railway line, beyond which rough pasture tumbled to the Ogwr Fach at the bottom of the valley. The back gardens of the Thomas Street houses also fell away precipitously to a brook, which ran parallel to the street, but they had a southerly aspect and Joan and Tom were nimble enough to cultivate vegetables on the slope. As almost everywhere in the valley, a comfortable, cheerful kitchen was the heart of the house. For a few years they took me on an annual outing to the pantomime in Cardiff, which I suppose I looked forward to and enjoyed. If I had been a hardier, rough and ready sort of boy, perhaps I would have visited them more often, and they might have found more time for me – at least until they started their own family. Kitty, black haired and tiny, was born in 1947. Presumably, the temporary separation my cousin Jean spoke of occurred before that. A second daughter, Pam, came in 1952, and a third, Vivien, four years later.

I recall dimly that Joan continued factory work, though not with munitions, probably once Kitty and Pam were in school and 'off her hands'. In any event, somewhere outside the home she caught TB, though not of the classic sort, for which by that time medical science had begun to find answers. In her case the bacteria struck the pericardium, the membrane enclosing the heart, beyond the reach of fresh air and pills. She was told that she must have swallowed the infection. The operation to cut out the affected part was delicate and dangerous so that she was a long time in hospital and her return to full health very slow. Because Joan was not strong enough, until she was three, her third daughter, Vivien, was very largely looked after by Barbara, who, with all her own troubles, still lived at home. Having gone up to Aberystwyth in 1952, I was barely aware of the seriousness of Joan's illness, though I was once shown part of the huge sickle-shaped scar that ran down her breastbone and curved away to the left under her ribs.

Who knows what prompted Joan and Tommy to take the tenancy of the Griffin Inn, a dilapidated, moribund pub off the main road from Tonyrefail as it neared the City crossroads? It was half a mile down a narrow dirt road, over a stubby hump-backed bridge that crossed a disused branch railway line. The building dated from the late nineteenth century, when it provided office and accommodation for the sinking of an unsuccessful and early abandoned pit nearby, the last evidence of which was a low mound of shale containing fragments of coal measures fossils. At a distance, the pub and its outhouses might be mistaken for a small farm at the bottom of a shallow valley. Negotiating the stone bridge into the car park demanded the close attention of motorists. On one occasion, a bus bearing a party on an outing became stuck astride the hump, its front wheels barely touching the road on the down side and back wheels in the air.

The brook, a haunt of newts and tadpoles, joins the River Ely in Tonyrefail, its first houses visible only a mile away down the valley. Where once were only fields, hedges and little unkempt clusters of trees, the main road has taken a fresh turn and new housing has appeared recently. In the other direction, the view is of hillsides – rough pasture to the left and fields enclosed by straggling hedges to the right. It is probably less than a mile from the top of Thomas Street and by no means remote, but especially on summer days, with the flock of birds picking and crooning in the yard, it could seem in the heart of the country, peacefully serene. Marshy ground round and about the brook gave the local name to the spot, 'the bog', which in turn became attached to the pub. If you speak of The Bog in Gilfach and neighbouring villages for miles around, people immediately understand you are referring to the Griffin Inn.

Joan and Tommy took the pub in 1962. They appeared from the start cut out for it, possessing that social ease, cheery briskness, and authority (when it came to setting and keeping standards of behaviour) that customers were comfortable with. They soon had enough regulars to keep the business going and increasingly over the years attracted drinkers from further afield who were not passing trade but had chosen to walk or drive down the rutted and potholed lane and over the bridge.

The cold, stone flagged cellar, where a constant trickle of water betrayed a spring that had found its way through the masonry, was Tommy's domain. My sister's interest in old furniture, china and bric-a-brac, given space to expand and a free rein, expressed itself in wooden settles, scores of plates and jugs on a high shelf around the bar, swords, a flintlock, a glowing, brass-buttoned Welsh Guards dress jacket and a variety of colourful trinkets. Many pieces were donated, some bought for a few shillings from refuse collectors, who put to one side any discarded objects they thought might interest her. The Bog was not really ancient but it acquired an aura of antiquity that customers enjoyed and felt at home in. Above all, it was a place for conversation: there was no jukebox or piped music, and no food was served. You went to The Bog for a quiet pint and a lively gossip. The police, who know good licensed premises when they see them, held occasional off-duty parties there after stop-tap.

In the mid-1980s Joan and Tommy bought the freehold of the pub and surrounding land from the brewery, part of a large leisure conglomerate. As a condition of the sale my sister (who had always been formally the licensee) was expected to surrender the licence. The brewery intended it should be taken up by a local entrepreneur, whom Joan described as 'shady', only more colourfully. He and the brewery planned a much bigger establishment, offering a wide range of entertainment, on waste land at the top of the lane. The Bog closed.

Whether what followed was planned from the outset, or occurred fortuitously, one thing leading to another, I do not know. It was certainly a shock to the brewery. At the magistrates' court hearing, Joan declared she would not surrender the licence and, since there had been no complaint about the running of the pub, that was that. The brewery took its case to the Crown Court in Cardiff. I was then working nearby in Cathays Park and at my lunch break I walked over to the court. Neither Joan nor Tommy was there, but a busload of their supporters had come to see justice done. At one memorable point, the judge suggested that a pub known as The Bog couldn't possibly be up to much. The mutinous rumble from the public benches visibly startled him. I left before the hearing ended, but at this point, any further moves planned by legal representatives of the giant corporation were cut short by a letter from the Office of Fair Trading, which said that a restrictive covenant of the kind included in its contract was illegal.

The Bog re-opened as a free house to widespread rejoicing. Tommy took pride in the reputation for a good pint, and now he added real ales with outlandish names from small independent breweries to the cask beers and lagers that are the norm these days. Twelve months later, in 1988, it was listed in the *Good Beer Guide* as 'an excellent old-fashioned pub'.

In time, Tommy, long retired from post office telephones, became scrawny, and his talk increasingly difficult to understand, though the gap-toothed smiles and winks for customers were as bright and wicked as ever. A stairlift was installed to carry him to the little-used sitting room and the bedrooms above the bar. He had Parkinson's. When he died Joan carried on, putting her face on each evening to preside over the bar where two of her daughters who lived locally were on hand to assist. These were the years when my calls became more frequent and we would pore together over unsorted piles of family photographs while Joan tried to put names to the faces of relatives, many long dead, who, if I ever knew them, I barely remembered.

During this time she broke her thigh without being aware of it other than as a persistent ache and, after having the fracture pinned, returned at once to the pub. For a day or two she used a stick, and then forgot about it. I had a message that she was in hospital with Legionnaires' disease. When I visited she was sitting up in bed peering with unnaturally large eyes at the roof visible through the ward window. 'Can you see those big birds?' she said. 'They're there all the time.' I surveyed the roof where there were no birds of any sort to be seen; nor was there a fire in the middle of the ward floor, which to her was menacingly present. Then she was well again, out in the yard among her real birds, or sitting on a low stool in the corner by the fire with the cats and dogs for company.

Joan had strongly-held, often reactionary, opinions about society and the world at large. She was straight and straight-talking – cheeky, some might have said, looking down at her. Having since childhood outrun a variety of deadly threats, she seemed indestructible, but at last insidious cancer caught up with her. She died in October 1999.

***

If in Joan the milk of human kindness could sometimes seem in short supply, in Barbara it flowed constantly and free. It was she who held together the threads of family. Sociable and caring, she maintained contact with those elements of my father's family who lived locally, most of whom I simply did not know. (I was sometimes an embarrassment to my parents and myself when word got back that I had passed by a cousin or uncle or aunt without greeting or sign of recognition. It was assumed I was 'stuck up'.) It was Barbara too who wrote, not often but regularly, to the scattered membership of my mother's family – all those aunts, uncles and cousins – so that we knew from year to year where and how they were. When she died, no one took on the role and, neglected, the network dissolved. The fault, I know, is mostly mine.

Babs was born in 1922, about twenty-one months after Joan. I shall never forget her birthday because it falls in November, two days before mine. Unlike Joan, she was a healthy child and was eventually taller by a few inches, though that is not saying a great deal. She was always affectionate and quick in perception and understanding, and bright too. Illness deprived Joan of many weeks of schooling and during this time Mama did what she could to teach her older daughter how to read. The younger one was a constant, close and silent eavesdropper on this activity and when it was her turn to go to school she surprised the teachers by being able to read on arrival. She was taken around classes of older children to show them how an infant could manage it, while some of them still could not.

A photograph of Babs as a girl, probably in her final year at the elementary school, shows her in wire-framed spectacles, round-faced, with bobbed hair, smiling. Five years later, in a cutting from the *Daily Herald*, dated 25 April 1939, she is very pretty young woman, aged sixteen, a little apprehensive, but smiling again for the press photographer, after having been chosen 'from a record number of entries' as May Queen of Gilfach. She had a wonderful wide smile, inherited from the Loves, my mother's family, while Joan, like Mam, my father's mother, had a small mouth, easily pursed in determination. In those days Babs loved to go out dancing. I imagine her in a crowd of friends, and in constant demand as a partner on the floor. There was a lightness about her, a fizz of energy.

Perhaps it was at a dance that she met Leighton. I have not the faintest memory of him, but I am certain we met sometime between 1939 and 1941. His fate drew us all into a long, dismal passage, in which Barbara suffered most cruelly.

Leighton was in the Royal Navy. A portrait photograph

shows him in the uniform of a naval rating, serious, arms folded, a handsome young man with frank blue eyes (the photograph has been tinted) and neatly parted wavy hair. On one sleeve is a badge that shows he is an anti-aircraft gunner. His ship, HMS *Repulse*, was a battle cruiser; it had a crew of more than 1,500. Before he returned to her for his last voyage he left with Barbara a photograph album that included a large formal picture of the entire ship's complement assembled on deck beneath the huge fifteen-inch guns. It was both impressive and moving: 'the many men, so beautiful'.

I do not have the album or any longer know where it is. When Joan offered it to me, I did not want it. But I know its contents well – groups of sailors, his friends, in tropical kit, great seas breaking over dipping bows, fancy dress and wild antics frozen in time at a 'crossing the line ceremony', views from the deck of cities and harbours visited. As a boy, from time to time I would go to the cupboard in the mirrored sideboard where the album was kept and surreptitiously take it out, not to look at these pleasant enough images of life in the peacetime navy in foreign parts, but drawn by a mixture of fascination and revulsion to pages containing a gallery of horrors from the Sino-Japanese War. There were a dozen or so snapshots of Japanese atrocities – torture, beheadings, black pools of blood around sundered bodies. I never became inured to its horrors; usually, in no more than a minute, I had seen enough and, with a sick guilt, would slip the album back into its place. If I close my eyes, I can see those pages still.

Barbara and Leighton married early in February 1941 in the corrugated sheeting clad 'Mission Church' at the bottom end of the valley, for the stone-built St Barnabas, a good deal nearer, was already bomb-damaged and out of commission. My father was one of the witnesses; Uncle Will, husband of my father's sister, Julia, the other. Leighton was obviously on leave, but the certificate gives him an address in Gilfach less than a hundred yards from our house, but not then his family home, for his father was not present at the ceremony.

Leighton's father, William 'Willy' Francis, was well known in Gilfach. He had been a musical prodigy, as a child playing the piano and the church organ when his hands were too small to stretch an octave. He married and settled for a time in Weymouth, where Leighton was born in 1919. I was told he became a pianist and bandleader on cruise ships. Photographs of rugby and hockey teams at Cowbridge School in the early 1930s (one of which includes Alun Lewis, the Welsh poet and short story writer) suggest Leighton was a boarder there, though for how long I cannot say.

His early experience of the Far East at the time of the Sino-Japanese War, which began in earnest in 1937, might possibly have been on another vessel, but the only ship pictured in his album is HMS *Repulse*, on which the majority of the crew were, like him, regular servicemen. His story from that point on is bound up with the history of the Second World War. He was probably on board during the initial stages of the hunt for the *Bismarck* in May 1941, when the *Repulse* was forced to return to port for refuelling before the action that resulted in the sinking of the German battleship. Later that same year, he was certainly part of the crew when the ship put to sea at Singapore in company with the *Prince of Wales* and an escort of four destroyers to strike at Japanese forces that had advanced through French Indo-China and, following landings in Thailand and Malaya, were moving south.

Britain had been at war with Japan since 7 December, and the heavy guns of the *Prince of Wales* and *Repulse* were intended to be a first response to aggression. The *Prince of Wales* was a new, heavily armoured battleship, pride of the British fleet; the *Repulse*, launched in 1916, had been through several refits, but did not have the same weight of armour or weaponry. Her two batteries of eight four-inch anti-aircraft guns, though dated, were capable of firing 960 two-inch rounds per minute, when operating perfectly. They were known onomatopoeically as pompoms. Each battery had a ten-man crew; Leighton was a member of one of these crews.

They sailed on 10 December. About 10 a.m. on 12 December, some 170 miles from Singapore, they were spotted by a Japanese reconnaissance plane. The history is precise. Seventy-three Japanese aircraft set out from bases near Saigon, fifty carrying torpedoes. By 11.15 a.m. the *Prince of Wales* had been hit by a torpedo and, its rudder damaged, was listing and turning slowly in circles. The *Repulse* had survived an initial bombing run more or less unscathed but problems with the ammunition meant that by the time of the first torpedo attack neither of the pompom batteries was working properly. Because the batteries were not enclosed in turrets, pompom gunners were particularly vulnerable and men had been killed and wounded by machine-gun fire from the aircraft. By manoeuvring the vessel to present the narrow target of the ship's bows, the commander had avoided fourteen torpedoes, but in a final wave of attacks from two sides she was struck five times in rapid succession. The effect was devastating and the ship sank within eight minutes at about midday. Wallowing helplessly, its guns out of action, the *Prince of Wales* followed soon after.

On the other side of the world, Mama was awakened by the sensation of a heavy blow to the chest and searing pain. In London, some hours later, Prime Minister Churchill, surrounded by red boxes, though still in bed, received the news by telephone with incredulity. He was assured it was all too true. He later wrote, 'In all the war I never received a more direct shock.'

The shock felt by the families and friends of seamen on the two ships, when the sketchy initial information was broadcast and newspapers took up the story, is barely imaginable, even in these days when we are almost daily reminded of the grief of those whose loved ones have died in combat overseas. I don't think it touched me; certainly I have no memory of sorrow, but for Barbara and my parents it must have been a terrible time and, after the official letter, 'missing, believed killed', such protracted torture. What value do you place on hope at times like that?

Some time in 1945, shortly before or after the end of the war, a sailor from the Rhondda, who had survived the sinking of the *Repulse*, called at the house. It may have been he who gave me the banana, a small bent thing, soft, black and heavily perfumed. It was so unlike any illustration of the fruit I had seen that I was deeply suspicious. The gift was not the reason for his unannounced visit. He had news to put an end to hope and waiting. He told Barbara that Leighton had been killed at his post by enemy aircraft machine-gunning the decks. He had been shot in the chest, as my mother had long known.

It was during the war years that my mother and Barbara became interested in spiritualism. They were not alone. Many thousands afflicted by the pain, grief and uncertainties of the time were looking desperately for reassurance and relief. And there were other reasons. Often in severe pain, my mother developed a heightened awareness of things beyond the physical, shocking at first, that we came to accept. No medical help then existed that could ease her suffering, far less cure the condition. It was not surprising that she looked elsewhere. Barbara needed Leighton, who was God knew where. And there was Leigh, Leighton's son, born in November 1941, shortly before his father was killed. He seemed a beautiful baby with fair curly hair, but he did not thrive. He slept and ate poorly. The black cocker spaniel pup we called Dinah, bought at this time, grew monstrously fat on the carefully prepared foods Leigh would not or could not eat. I don't know how old he was when he suffered the first convulsion – a year, fifteen months perhaps, because he had begun to walk. I saw enough of them later, when he could have several in a day. Terrible paroxysms would seize him without warning and he would fall to the floor, his whole body jerking and flailing, and there was nothing anyone could do until the fit had left him exhausted.

Was it any wonder that copies of *Psychic News* accumulated in one of the sideboard cupboards, or that Barbara wrote regularly to Harry Edwards the 'absent healer'? It did no good. Leigh never walked steadily but had a stumbling run and was usually frenetically active. The only respite came when he was asleep, but he slept little and was easily disturbed. As he grew older, within the house, which was his whole world (he rarely went out after early perambulator days), all unknowing, he related to things about him destructively, slamming the doors of rooms and any cupboard within his reach, and violently tipping over chairs with an appearance of intense glee, then colliding with furniture, falling, hurting himself. His limbs were thin and he looked frail, but he was strong. I do not recall he ever said 'Mam' or 'Mama'; his only speech was 'eeee', learned early joining in our mother's repeated 'One, two, three'. Even at this distance of time, to think of Barbara's loss and the toil and hopelessness motherhood brought her is infinitely sad. Then, there was no pause for thought. For her and Mama, constant care and work filled each day and often the night hours.

One of my clearest childhood memories is of a caravan holiday at Porthcawl with Barbara and Leigh when he was a still a baby. The weather was cool, dull and showery; perhaps it was late August. Barbara did not go far from the caravan, but if it were dry, I would visit a particular pool I had found on the rocky foreshore, which I stocked with sea anemones, hermit crabs and any other creatures I could pluck from neighbouring pools, until I had created a colourful world refreshed by every tide. And once, near this pool, I found a blunted pyramid of stone with a metal ring attached that fitted in my palm. An angler who had a pitch nearby declared it was a deep-sea fishing weight and gave me two shillings for it. This cultivation of a sea-garden, was a deep, if lonely, pleasure, but not the intention of the holiday. I was probably meant to help my sister in the caravan; I hope I did.

At home, I would be asked to look after Leigh in the back

room, the smaller of the downstairs sitting rooms, while Mama and Babs gathered their strength with a cup of tea and a cigarette. It was a task I undertook with ill grace and carelessly. And from time to time I took him to bed in the evening and tried to get him to sleep. I would lock my arms and legs around him and hold him while he squirmed and fought against my grasp. At last, worn out, he would lie still and eventually fall asleep. If I were patient and lucky, I would disentangle myself without stirring him and creep downstairs. But he never slept long. I wonder now how my sister managed, always sleeping with her wakeful child, because he could not be left alone. He was five or six when the place was found for him at Hensol, a hospital for 'mental defectives' as people with learning disabilities were then known. There he died, aged twenty-one, in the summer of 1963. In all those years, although he could not recognise her and did not know one day from the next, Barbara visited him every Wednesday. Once only, in my early teens, I went with her for company: three bus changes to meet such visions of deformity, unalleviated by cheer or hope, and three bus changes back.

She was young, barely in her mid-twenties, and very attractive, when Leigh was taken in at Hensol. With her responsibilities at home much reduced, though our mother's health was rapidly declining, she began to go out in the evenings. Usually it was to help behind the bar at the Con Club, which was only twenty yards away across the road from our house. Since her marriage to Leighton, Babs had rarely, if ever, gone out other than to the shops for groceries, so tied was she by pregnancy, war widowhood and the handicapped child she had borne. She was by nature sociable and engaging, but had suppressed her instincts. Learning how to pull pints without waste, and doing it quickly when there was a rush at the bar, learning how to calculate the cost of rounds of drinks and give change without loss to the till, learning to take the banter of men with a smile, and where to draw the line, were all exciting. At stop tap she would come home flushed and happy, more fully alive than she had been in years.

It was probably at the Con she met Allan Davies. It is easy to understand how he fell for her, and he was a manly sort of man, broad and burly, with a long, oval face, dark, wavy hair and a big smile. He came from Tonyrefail, had a large circle of friends and enjoyed spending his evenings drinking and playing darts. He usually carried his own darts, heavy and shaped like miniature bombs, which he hurled hard and accurately, so that they struck the board with three resounding thumps. From time to time, when disagreements arose in bar or lounge and offence was given and taken, there might be a fight. Allan could handle himself in these situations; his fists flew as hard and accurately as his darts. During the war he had served with the RAF in besieged Malta, when the island was under constant bombardment from the air – a time of great personal privation and danger – and had come through it relatively unscathed.

If he had not courted Babs, I doubt I should ever have met him. His conversation consisted largely of descriptions of public bar characters and incidents, but that had become familiar territory to me, and having got to know him, if only slightly, I thought him agreeable enough. My parents did not share that view. Dada had made enquiries about Allan and what he learned was not reassuring: he was known as a regular about the pubs and clubs, where some of those he mixed with were crude and offensive (a common enough case).

My mother formed an instant dislike of him that did not change as the years passed. Whenever he visited our house, Dada would be coolly polite, but Mama would hasten to another room, if she could manage it, without exchanging a word. Looking back, it is not easy to justify their behaviour. I am sure Allan loved Barbara (how else could he have put up with the way their relationship was circumscribed?) and, I believe, would never have harmed her, but to my parents he was an undesirable. Perhaps, too, they feared he would take her away from them (though they would have denied this), for she had become the engine of the household and its connection with the world. It was she who dusted every morning, making the elaborate drawer handles on the sideboard rattle, and vacuumed vigorously; and she who went shopping and brought back the valley's gossip. But my mother's rule was law and if she would not have Allan in the house, the most he could hope for was a brief call to pick up Babs and take her out for the evening. Eventually they had a car for outings, bought with the help of a small bequest in the will of Leighton's father.

When Muriel and I married in October 1958, Allan was my best man, which pleased Barbara. My parents did not attend the wedding in Tonypandy; my mother, wheelchair bound, could not have managed it no matter how heartily she wished, and there was no question of Dada being there without her. The following summer, Barbara and Allan came to spend a weekend with us in Bristol, where we had set up our first home in a flat above a grocer's shop. Unsure how to accommodate them, we made preparations for them to sleep separately, using the bed settee in the sitting room and a second bedroom. Shortly after their arrival, Allan told us that so far as sleeping was concerned there was no problem: they were married.

Was this a shock? I am not sure. It was certainly a surprise, but so far as I recall we did not take it amiss. They had married secretly in 1953, but continued to live separately as before. Ever mindful of her duty of care as a daughter, Barbara would not leave home, and she accepted that my mother would not countenance Allan living under the same roof. Five years on, my parents still knew nothing of the marriage and Barbara was determined as ever not to tell them. Allan followed her lead. Joan knew, for she had been a witness at the register office wedding, but she, too, remained silent – as we did thereafter. At length, Dada might possibly have guessed or heard a rumour, but whatever suspicion he may have had, he did not share with my mother. She found out in the autumn of 1964, when Allan, who was diabetic, died in a coma and police came looking for next of kin. My mother, who was in the house alone, answered the door with the usual difficulty. Was Mrs Davies there they wanted to know. No, they must have the wrong house. 'Mrs Barbara Davies', they persisted, and the penny dropped. The story of Barbara and Allan, romantic or pathetic, seems not to belong to twentieth-century industrial south Wales, but to a distant time and place, in which lover and beloved are kept apart by unjust fate.

Allan worked as a school caretaker, perhaps because the job provided accommodation as well as a wage. Apart from evenings with Barbara or drinking at a nearby club, he led a lonely life. He paid scant regard to his diabetic condition and was only forty-five when he died.

Our parents were not vindictive; they were loving and protective, perhaps especially of Barbara, who had already suffered much. One day during the war years she returned from the Co-op in tears. She had asked Vaughan the butcher for something extra and he had snarled at her, as he well knew how because he was a bully to his wife, in front of a crowd of shoppers. Didn't she know there was a war on? The butcher, supposed a friend, had frequently availed himself of our hospitality and his bluster, real or feigned, hurt and embarrassed her badly. My father was told when he came in from work. Still black from the pit he went to the Co-op and before another crowd of spectators swore to Vaughan that if ever his daughter was spoken to again as she had been that morning he would need more than a cleaver to save him from the hiding he would surely get. The butcher quailed.

We were still living in Bristol, the children at nursery by day, both Muriel and I teaching, and information from Gilfach and Tonypandy reached us slowly. Our house in Fishponds did not have a telephone, but we usually had an exchange of news with our families by phoning from a nearby kiosk at weekends and that, presumably, was how we heard about

Allan. I cannot say we were deeply saddened by his death; he had not featured prominently in our lives and we did not miss him. Nor do I know how it affected Barbara, whose grief may well have been mitigated by their unusual marital arrangements. For several years she had worked regularly in a shop a hundred yards or so up the road which sold radios and television sets, gramophone records and a variety of small electrical items. The shop was owned by Glyn Jones, who was happy to allow his employee a measure of flexibility in her working hours, as long as she could be on hand while he was out attending to the repair work that was an important part of the business. As Mama became more capable of cooking, washing and answering the door from her wheelchair, so work in the shop became more engrossing and enjoyable for Barbara. She was a good at selling, a gift she may have inherited from our grandfather.

Glyn was an interesting character, with a certain insouciant charm. He wore a trilby indoors as much as out because he was almost completely bald, but had a pleasant face with a finely shaped nose, wide mouth and broad, thin-lipped smile. He had many interests, and as a skilled electrician spoke the same language as my father. He had been only seventeen at the beginning of the war, but was soon conscripted. As a member of the 'Forgotten Army', he fought against the Japanese in the jungles of Burma, a campaign in which, for every battle casualty, 120 were evacuated with sickness. It was an appalling conflict: official reports tell that of the 26,000 men who died, 20,000 have no known graves. In the course of a campaign involving swiftly moving 'long columns', he was one of those who fell so desperately ill that he was left by his comrades to die or survive as fate decreed. He remembered iridescent insects, like jewels, flying and creeping about him and nothing more until he recovered consciousness in a friendly native village where he was cared for until chance once more brought a British detachment within reach and, somewhat recovered, he was handed back. He had married after the war but not happily, and the near presence of Barbara, still young and vivacious, in his shop may have been less than helpful to a deteriorating relationship.

Glyn was welcomed by my parents as Allan had never been and with Barbara widowed for a second time and his own marriage beyond repair, their relationship prospered, despite the continuing complications of a wife unwilling to divorce. The details of what followed escape me, but with Dada's death in the spring of 1971, and I suppose, a divorce finalised at last, they married in 1976. They lived in a comfortable terraced house in Tonyrefail, where Glyn had another shop selling electrical items, to which Barbara gradually added a variety of fancy goods. I had never known my sister happier. When our boys were about eleven or twelve, while Muriel and I attended Welsh summer schools at Coleg Harlech, they holidayed happily in Tonyrefail with Glyn and Barbara.

Babs and Glyn had a business they both enjoyed, Joan's pub as a local and many friends. Lifting and carrying the monstrously heavy television sets of that era had damaged Glyn's back, but they had reached a plateau of contentment, perhaps without recognising it. The notion of moving to Torquay came out of the blue. They had visited the town and thought it beautiful, as, compared objectively with Tonyrefail, it probably is. They had information about an off-licence for sale on the hill above the town centre and sea front and decided this was what they wanted. The lease of the Tonyrefail shop was sold and they found a buyer for the house. The off-licence was not on a busy thoroughfare but had a clientele of locals that kept things ticking over. From the previous owners they inherited Tilly, an enormous rottweiler, to deter unwelcome customers and thieves, and seemed settled – but not for long.

A mortgage survey of the house in Tonyrefail revealed cracks in the structure and the building society refused to lend the money the buyer needed to complete the purchase. Without the proceeds of the house sale Babs and Glyn were unable to pay off the bridging loan they had taken out to buy the off-licence. They were a long way from Tonyrefail, with a business to run, and felt they had no option but to leave the problem to their solicitor there, who sat on his hands. It was several months before, in the course of a visit to Torquay, we were told of this apparently intractable problem. Of course, the house in Ton was insured, which meant that if the cracks could be shown to be caused by subsidence the insurer would pay for the necessary remedial work, and a buyer would be able to obtain a mortgage on it.

For once I was able to help Barbara, who had done so much for me throughout my childhood and youth. The solicitor was glad to relinquish his responsibilities. It was a simple matter to contact the insurer and then the insurer's surveyor and discover precisely what was needed to allow him to certify that subsidence had or had not occurred. He wanted a hole a couple of feet square and deep enough to expose the foundations, two or three feet down he thought would be plenty. My niece Vivien's then husband, a burly fellow, used to handling pick and shovel, completed the modest excavation in ten minutes; the surveyor turned up at the hour appointed, looked briefly at the sagging bricks below ground level and declared, yes, it was subsidence and he would report accordingly. The house was re-advertised but because Glyn was now desperate to sell, it fetched a lower price than he had originally expected.

Not long after, on another visit, Barbara complained of a pain in her back, which all the usual over-the-counter drugs seemed unable to shift. She found relief only in a hot water bottle pressed to the place. Eventually she was referred to a consultant who diagnosed pancreatic cancer. Nothing could be done. During the May half-term holiday the following year, 1983, Muriel spent a week caring for her, watching her fade. Soon after, she died. When I saw her white coffin, small as a child's coffin, I wept.

Glyn sold up and returned to south Wales, finding a house in Beddau, another mining village (the location of Cwm Colliery, where my father had spent his last working years).

Although he occasionally came up to the Bog and put on a show of cheerfulness, with Tilly as his only companion, he became increasingly reclusive. He was inconsolable, totally lost, not caring how or whether he lived. Eventually, not having seen him for a while, neighbours forced an entry and found him unconscious. As he was being carried to the ambulance, the dog, so old she could hardly drag her great weight about, collapsed and died. In hospital, Glyn survived a week or so without recovering consciousness. His was a case, if ever there was one, of a broken heart. Because there was no one else to do the job, Vivien and Pam, my nieces, cleared the house, which they found in a state of dreadful neglect, apart from one bedroom where there were two wardrobes filled with Barbara's clothes, everything neatly hung or stored in drawers as though waiting for her, and still holding the faint remembrance of her perfume.

Epilogue

ALTHOUGH I DIDN'T realise it at the time, when, in September 1952, aged seventeen, I went up to Aberystwyth, I was beginning to leave home. The bonds of family, of love and shared experience were very strong, but I felt no homesickness, no sense of disorientation or loss. It was partly because I trusted my mother, father and sister, and the house, to stay just as I had left them, as indeed they did. Every week I posted home an account of my student life; every week I had a reply. I also sent home laundry, as there was no provision in digs for washing clothes, nor was there a laundrette in Aberystwyth in those days. Neatly-packed, clean clothes returned promptly accompanied by Welsh cakes or pasties from our kitchen. I thought of them as Red Cross parcels and was torn between the temptation to devour the tastes of home at once and with delight, or eke them out as best I could over a few days. I had carried my ration book with me to Aber and, even if I had had the money to buy, post-war shops had little to offer.

The journey between Gilfach Goch and Aberystwyth involved transport by four different bus companies and took from 8.30 a.m. to 4 p.m. Going home during the term was out of the question and never entered my thoughts, but the excitement of returning for Christmas or Easter or the long summer vacation never diminished. It was always wonderful to be there and feel the walls close around me and the warmth of good coal fires and love within. But, apart from the summer term, with examinations in prospect, it was not difficult to leave again. Aberystwyth had become another life and, after six years, I would happily have committed myself to being a student forever.

I was on holiday after graduation in the summer of 1955

when I met Muriel at a Saturday dance in The Library, Llwynypia. She lived nearby in Blaenclydach, not far from the crowded terraces where my mother's family had lived in the 1900s, and was about to start a college course in Bristol. Red Rhondda buses plying between Tonypandy Square and Gilfach Goch kept us physically in touch during vacations and when apart we wrote. During the second year of research at Aber, my first task most days in the college library was to write to Muriel. We decided to marry and, thesis submitted, I was fortunate to be appointed to a teaching post in Bristol (where she was already teaching) on the very last school day of the summer term 1958. We married the following October half-term and found the flat above Garrett's grocer's shop in Eastville, more or less equidistant from Muriel's school in Fishponds and mine at Lockleaze.

Bristol to Gilfach by train and bus was easier and quicker than the journey from Aber had been, and occasionally on Friday afternoons we joined the crowd of teachers on the platform at Stapleton Road Station bound for south Wales. But soon there were things to be done at weekends that kept us in Bristol, not least school preparation and marking, and I began playing rugby regularly. We went home during school holidays. It was always 'home', although we were withdrawing from it and building a separate life. Our first son, Nicholas, was born in Bristol in April 1960. I had bought an entirely unsuitable small sports car and, on a sunny day, collected mother and child from the maternity home with the roof down. Jonathan was born at the flat over the shop in July 1961. In the spring of 1962, Muriel withdrew her teachers' superannuation contributions and with a loan of £50 from my father we were able to make the down payment on a three-bedroom 1930s semi-detached in Fishponds. I never repaid the loan.

The early 1960s saw a great increase in the numbers of young school-age children and a shortage of teachers for them. The headmistress of the school where Muriel had previously taught with distinction, which was within easy walking distance of our house, came to ask if she would return; there were nursery places for our children. So she resumed teaching, and Nicholas and Jonathan (although he was only two) went with her. It was a very busy time for all of us, but we were healthy and happy, and for the first time I began to realise how lucky I was. During school holidays we went to Gilfach; I don't think it ever occurred to us to go anywhere else. We were welcomed into the warmth of the old house as before, filling it now for our stay with the paraphernalia young children require. A photograph from this time has my mother in the doorway of the back room with the boys – Jonathan, about eighteen months, and Nicholas, almost three, close to her. It is sunny and the photograph is over exposed, but the faces are clear enough; my mother is smiling.

It was a time of rapid expansion and staff turnover in comprehensive schools and within five years at Lockleaze I had become head of the English department. After three more years I was ready to move on and in 1966 I became a lecturer in English at Caerleon College of Education. At the same time Muriel was appointed to the infants' school in the village. Our journeys from Bristol had involved a drive along the Severn estuary as far as Gloucester and then down the other side, or an uncertain wait for the Aust ferry that, if we managed to get on, would drop us unceremoniously near Chepstow. In August that year when the Severn Bridge, which we had long observed under construction, opened, we were back in south Wales. We bought a house in a new development on a ridge above the valley of the Afon Llwyd, overlooking Ponthir. We were within an hour's drive of Gilfach Goch and the Rhondda.

Early the following October I received a message at the college to say my mother was seriously ill. She was unconscious when I arrived and died soon after. Dada and Barbara went on living in the house and we continued to visit. The welcome was much the same until my father died in April 1971. I am glad our boys were old enough to have some faint memories of those times. What I have tried to do is to make them a gift of my memories to help fix and add to theirs, and pass on to their children.

Last August, during a rare spell of dry weather, I took our grandchildren to Gilfach. We stopped across the road from the house to see how it had changed: the grassed slope of the front lawn shrub covered, modern 'picture' windows, less distinguished in appearance, and probably less draughty, than those they replaced. We parked the car in Glamorgan Terrace, properly surfaced at last, near the house where Mama Love once lived with Aunty Lil and wheezing Uncle Percy, and we walked up the mountain behind the terrace, and climbed further until we could look down on all the upper part of the valley. It is beautiful again, no vestige of its mining past remaining. I had a few old photographs to show them how it had been when I was a boy and three working pits and mountains of slag filled the valley floor. And there was the constant noise of men working and steam engines pulled long lines of trucks empty up the valley and heaped with coal down and away.

Acknowledgements

FOR MOST OF what appears in this book I am indebted to memory. But memory, I know, is a faulty instrument, especially when it involves people and events in the distant past, and anecdotes that have been told and retold many times, including some that were, in any case, received second hand. I freely admit, also, to speculation about certain relationships when prolonged searching has failed to unearth clinching evidence. It is just as well in the circumstances that I have been able to obtain, from a variety of sources, a measure of factual rigour as framework and backbone to what might otherwise have been dismissed as wishful thinking.

Census and other relevant data of births, deaths and marriages are available online and I have plundered these for a decade or more, long before I ever thought of gathering what I had learned into a book. For more specific guidance in this quest I owe a great deal to J. Barry Davies, an expert in family history and friend of many years, and, more recently, to Gwyn Rhys of the Glamorgan Family History Society. I read the eighteenth-century diary of John Perkins, a farmer in the Vale of Glamorgan, at the library of St Fagans National History Museum, and obtained entirely unexpected and revelatory documentary evidence about ancestors in the eighteenth century from the archive service of the National Library of Wales.

All the information about the Jones family who once owned Merthyr Mawr comes from Glamorgan Archives in Cardiff. Contemporary reports of family and other matters have been drawn from newspaper archives, particularly those of the *Cambrian* at Swansea, which luckily for me began publishing in 1804. Information has also come swiftly on request from archivists at the Worshipful Society of Apothecaries and the Victoria and Albert Museum in London, and from All Souls and Jesus College, Oxford. *Archaeologia Cambrensis* No. LI, July 1867, told me about the Plas and Church at Llantrithyd, while information about the Aubrey family was found in *Sir John Aubrey 1739–1826* by John Aubrey-Fletcher.

I owe an enormous debt of gratitude to the scholarly work of Kenneth O. Morgan, John Davies, Gwyn A. Williams and Dai Smith for the layman's knowledge I possess of Welsh history *circa* 1750–1950: I hope I have used it fairly and accurately. Any errors are certainly my own.

Information about slavery and other factors in the West Indies is taken from *Statistics of the Colonies of the British Empire* by R. M. Martin (W. H. Allen & Co., 1839). Descriptions of the valley and village of my boyhood are supplemented in a number of instances by material obtained from Katie Olwen Pritchard's *The Story of Gilfach Goch* (1973) and Meirion Davies's valuable *Glynogwr and Gilfach Goch: a history* (1981).

Quotations from 'Gwalia Deserta' and 'The Angry Summer' were taken from *The Collected Poems of Idris Davies*, edited by Islwyn Jenkins (Gomer, 1972). Song lyrics are from memory, but John Bunyan is credited with the words of 'To be a Pilgrim'. 'Thora', dating from 1905, was composed by Stephen Adams (not a relative) to words by Fred E. Weatherly, and Billy Reid wrote both words and music of 'Coming Home'.

A few of the 'historical' chapters have been adapted from my 'Letter from Wales' column in the Carcanet Press magazine *PN Review*, edited by Michael Schmidt, and the Ford Madox Ford quotations are from his *War Prose* edited by Max Saunders (Carcanet, 1999). Others' memories of Gilfach Goch are available on the web thanks to the activities of the Evanstown and Gilfach Goch Historical Society.

The little I know of life as a collier underground I owe to Vernon Harding of Coedely, who was endlessly patient in answering my questions. The photographs of Gilfach in the industrial era were given by Wyndham Jones from his own collection on behalf of the E&GGHS and Reflective Images of Taibach, Port Talbot. To the companions of my boyhood, some no longer with us, I can only say thanks for the memories.

Most special thanks I give to my wife, Muriel, patient first reader of all my writing, and to my editor, Eifion Jenkins.

About the author

SAM ADAMS WAS born and brought up in Gilfach Goch, Glamorgan, when it was a busy mining valley, his elementary school days there coinciding with the Second World War. Having studied English at the University College of Wales, Aberystwyth, he combined a career in education with work as writer and editor. His poems and critical writing have appeared in all the magazines of Welsh writing in English and he has made more than a hundred contributions to the Carcanet Press magazine *PN Review*. His editorial work includes the *Collected Poems* and *Collected Stories* of Roland Mathias and among his other publications are three monographs in the Writers of Wales series, three collections of poems and the novel *Prichard's Nose*.

Also by the author:

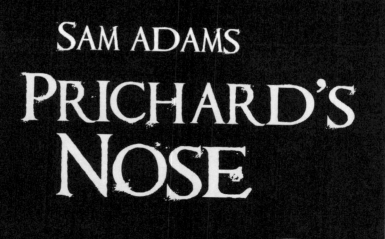

SAM ADAMS

PRICHARD'S NOSE

'... a remarkably vivid reconstruction of rural
Wales and London's theatreland in the 1800s
– and the perplexing puzzle of a lost nose'

Meic Stephens

y Lolfa

£9.95

SAM ADAMS

Missed Chances

y Lolfa

£5.95

Also from Y Lolfa:

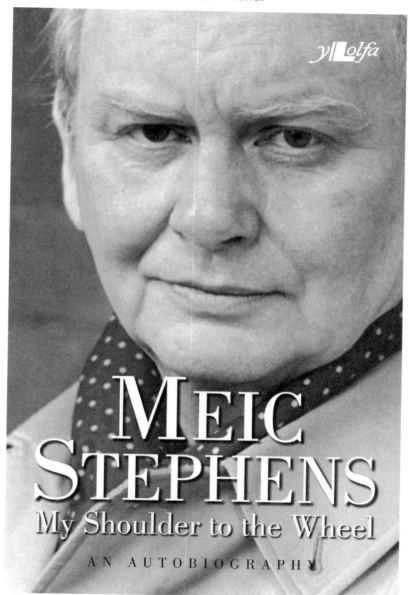

MEIC STEPHENS
My Shoulder to the Wheel
AN AUTOBIOGRAPHY

£9.95

Where the Stream Ran Red is just one of a
whole range of publications from Y Lolfa.
For a full list of books currently in print, send
now for your free copy of our new full-colour
catalogue. Or simply surf into our website

www.ylolfa.com

for secure on-line ordering.

TALYBONT CEREDIGION CYMRU SY24 5HE
e-mail ylolfa@ylolfa.com
website www.ylolfa.com
phone (01970) 832 304
fax 832 782